LOCAL GOVERNMENT DECENTRALISATION AND COMMUNITY

RECENT DISCUSSION PAPERS AVAILABLE FROM PSI

Policing and the Community (DP16)
Edited by PETER WILLMOTT
Discusses the development of community policing as part of the more general trend to introduce notions of community into policy and practice.

Debate About Community (DP13)
ALAN WALKER, PAUL EKBLOM & NICHOLAS DEAKIN (Edited by Peter Willmott)
Papers from a seminar on community in social policy.

Community and Social Policy (DP9)
PETER WILLMOTT with DAVID THOMAS
A review of the use of concepts of community, with interim conclusions about relevance to policy and suggestions on forms of further inquiry.

A full list of PSI Publications is available on request.

LOCAL GOVERNMENT DECENTRALISATION AND COMMUNITY

Edited by Peter Willmott

Policy Studies Institute

PSI Discussion Paper No. 18

PSI Publications are obtainable from all good bookshops, or by visiting the
Institute at 100 Park Village East, London NW1 3SR (01-387 2171)

Sales Representation: Pinter Publishers Ltd.
Mail and bookshop orders to: Marston Book Services,
                             P.O. Box 87,
                             Oxford OX4 1LB

ISBN 0-85374-414-9

Published by Policy Studies Institute
100 Park Village East, London NW1 3SR
Printed by Bourne Offset Ltd.

CONTENTS

CONTRIBUTORS

Robin Hambleton, Administrator and Special Lecturer, School of Advanced Urban Studies, University of Bristol

Liz du Parcq, Decentralisation Coordinator, Chief Executive's Department, London Borough of Islington

Peter Arnold, Principal Lecturer in Social Policy, Humberside College of Higher Education

Ian Cole, Principal Lecturer in Housing, Sheffield City Polytechnic

Bob Davies, formerly Coordinator, Community Networks, Birmingham, and now Chief Executive's Department, Birmingham City Council

John Gyford, Lecturer, University College London

Nicholas Deakin, Professor of Social Policy and Administration, University of Birmingham

Peter Willmott, Senior Fellow, Policy Studies Institute

DISCUSSANTS

Ken Young, formerly Senior Fellow, Policy Studies Institute, and now Director of Local Government Studies, University of Birmingham

Ken Spencer, Associate Director, Institute of Local Government Studies, University of Birmingham

Charles Barker, Assistant Director of Social Services, Thameside Metropolitan Borough,

Howard Elcock, Professor of Government, Newcastle-upon-Tyne Polytechnic

1 INTRODUCTION
Peter Willmott

These papers were originally given at a seminar at the Policy Studies Institute in March 1987. The seminar was part of a broader review of the relevance to policy of notions about community and neighbourhood. That work is supported by the Joseph Rowntree Memorial Trust (JRMT), and the seminar was chaired by Sir Charles Carter, Vice-Chairman of JRMT and Chairman of a recent JRMT working party which examined how to improve relations between central and local government [1].

The initiatives taking place in Britain under community or neighbourhood labels are a strange collection. Some — the community charge is an example — may seem to be just exploiting the modish terminology. The others have a wide range of objectives and methods. I would, however, argue that there are some common threads. I have elsewhere suggested that what has been happening in recent decades in this country, and indeed in most other western societies as well, can be seen as a reaction against the scale and remoteness of institutions both public and private [2]. The Barclay Report on the future of social work described the broad trend as 'a very general movement away from centralism and towards a belief in ordinary people' [3]. The approach is manifested in initiatives as diverse as community architecture and community policing [4]. It clearly underlies much of what is happening not only in local authority social services but in local government more generally, where the decentralisation is to local levels below that at which councils themselves operate.

The aim of the seminar, as with others at PSI, was to bring together people who had studied the subject and people who had experience of it in practice. The hope was to draw out some general conclusions about developments and give some guidance about the way ahead.

Local government decentralisation is itself a broad subject. For the purpose of the seminar it was narrowed down, and this is reflected in the papers collected here. They do not, for instance, deal with the financial implications or with the role of the unions, both of which are clearly important. The papers were intended to give particular attention to how residents are affected, in terms of service delivery, as members of community and voluntary groups and as citizens of a democracy.

The papers

The first paper, by Robin Hambleton, draws upon the work he has been doing with Paul Hoggett [5] and provides a general account of what is going on. As he shows, the trend to decentralisation — evident in the private sector as well — is gaining rather than losing momentum. At the same time the picture is one of great diversity. Different authorities, and to some extent authorities with different political complexions, give decentralisation different emphases or are even trying to do different things. Some approach it from the viewpoint of the consumers of council services, others lay particular stress on improving the management of services locally. Some see the objective as overcoming political apathy — 'political regeneration', as Ian Cole and Peter Arnold put it [6] — others as encouraging participation or even devolving some decision-making. The diversity is so great that it sometimes seems a mistake to call it all by the same name. Robin Hambleton draws out such variations and imposes an intelligible order on the complexity.

As his paper indicates, however, a broad distinction can be made between, on the one hand, attempts to improve services to council consumers through local delivery and, on the other, attempts to move towards a more participatory style of democracy. The other papers in this collection move from one to the other. Three are mainly about service delivery, one about the implications for residents not as individual consumers but as members of voluntary and community groups, and one about the general issue of decentralisation and democracy.

Liz du Parcq, the Decentralisation Coordinator for the London Borough of Islington, describes and assesses that council's decentralisation programme, with its network of neighbourhood offices. Though she is understandably disposed to find the Islington experience generally successful, she is frank about the difficulties. She acknowledges, for example, that the devolution of *power* has so far met with more suspicion than enthusiasm from residents, and that there are serious obstacles to overcome on that front. But, in terms of services, she shows that some measurable improvements have resulted from the localisation of offices and from more effective local coordination. The speed of repairs on council estates has increased and backlogs in processing housing benefit have been reduced. As for social services, the demand for their support has gone up, particularly in areas formerly distant from social services offices and, though there is no firm evidence about consumer satisfaction, she reports that impressions are favourable.

Ian Cole, discussing the decentralisation of housing services, argues that some Labour local authorities in particular have seen it as offering a means to counter the current onslaught on public housing. If the council stock could be managed in a less bureaucratic and less centralised fashion, more responsive to tenants' needs and wishes, there would be less of a case for breaking up council empires and transferring the property to housing associations, private trusts and the like. These interests are reflected in the sample survey quoted; there is more emphasis on improving services than decentralising power.

Cole is constrained in trying to arrive at an assessment of achievements and failures by the limitations of the evidence. Only a minority of councils in the survey were monitoring the impact of decentralisation and those who were confined themselves mainly to measures of the kinds cited by Liz du Parcq — the proportion of empty properties, speed of repairs, extent of arrears and the like. As well as generally lamenting this neglect, his main complaint is that, given that the aim is more contented tenants, it is disappointing that only a handful of authorities have systematically tried to canvass their views.

Peter Arnold, discussing some of the conceptual and methodological problems of assessing the decentralisation of social services, also laments the shortage of hard evidence. Drawing attention to the diversity in social services decentralisation, he argues that insufficient attention has been given to the political, professional and managerial implications and consequences. By way of guidance for the future, he notes some of the weaknesses in such evaluation as has been so far attempted.

Bob Davies's paper is a case study of decentralisation in Birmingham, and of how it has affected the City's voluntary and community groups. He makes some useful distinctions between different types of body: some are local, some are not; some are representative, some are campaigning bodies, some provide services. Their relationship with the local authority, locally and centrally, and their view of decentralisation, will vary according to their role and function. In any event he describes the context as an unpropitious one: though the City Council's local committees (which do not yet, as planned, include coopted residents) have made some important decisions affecting local people, in his view they lack the power and financial resources to have a significant impact. His general conclusion is that decentralisation in Birmingham has been constrained by traditional bureaucratic and centralist thinking, and that the potential contribution of the voluntary and community sector has been largely ignored.

John Gyford emphasises that in general it is easier to use decentralisation as a means to improve local service delivery than to devolve power. One extension of democracy which can work successfully is 'user control' — or more accurately in most cases, I would suggest, 'user participation'. The examples he gives are the involvement of tenants in managing their housing estate or parents their children's day nursery. Gyford concludes that this kind of participation, in the running of services that directly affect local people, may be 'a more promising avenue' than that of a broader neighbourhood-based democracy. In general, he is sceptical about more ambitious schemes, partly because of what he sees as an unwillingness on the part of politicians to give up their powers.

Nicholas Deakin, in his concluding comments, raises a disturbing question about the decentralisation measures introduced in the 1960s and 1970s — mini town halls, community development and neighbourhood councils are the examples he cites, and Robin Hambleton's paper mentions others. Why are those earlier experiments so comprehensively ignored? This is a point to which I return later. He also looks sceptically at residents' views of decentralisation, suggesting that their interest is limited, and arguing that what is happening is in any event fairly irrelevant to fundamental issues of resources, poverty, homelessness and race. He concludes, nevertheless, that decentralisation remains of potential importance, and his speculations about how it might develop in the future focus attention on the major questions to be answered.

The purposes of decentralisation

The papers and the seminar discussion based on them raise a number of such key issues. The first set are concerned with the objectives of decentralisation and the prospects of achieving them, the second with questions of scale, the third with the implications of decentralising for staff and councillors, and the fourth with monitoring and evaluation.

In any particular local authority the motives to decentralise, and to do so in one way rather than another, are influenced by local circumstances. The decisions may reflect the perceived pressures from and needs of consumers and voters, like those in Islington mentioned by Liz du Parcq. They may result from the personal convictions — or the personal ambitions — of particular politicians or chief officers. They may derive from political ideologies, as John Gyford's paper illustrates. But apart from these specific triggers, and despite the differences in emphasis among decentralising authorities, the two main objectives, as already noted, are to deliver services more effectively and to give people more say in the decisions affecting their lives.

With service delivery, it is worth asking how far the accessibility, quality and speed of services depend on decentralisation and how far they can be achieved by other means. The various anxieties and qualifications made by Peter Arnold and Ian Cole also need to be borne in mind [7]. But the Islington experience, and that of the Priority Estates Project [8] and the council estate schemes of the Safe Neighbourhoods Unit [9], suggest that decentralisation can lead to improvements in delivery, particularly in housing and social services. But that does not prove that decentralisation is the only way to obtain those improvements.

The other main aim of decentralisation is apparently more difficult to achieve. The difficulties of sharing power with residents through forums or area committees are suggested by Liz du Parcq's evidence from Islington and Bob Davies's from Birmingham, and are underlined by John Gyford. More limited and immediate versions, such as user control or user participation, can be successfully and usefully implemented. This has, however, so far been done at least as often outside councils' decentralisation programmes as within them, as witness for example the involvement of tenants in the housing estate projects just mentioned.

There is also everything to be said for local consultation and, where appropriate, negotiation when councils are preparing specific proposals affecting people's lives. Examples are a traffic management scheme, the building of a day nursery and the opening of a group home for people with mental handicaps. If residents and other interested groups are consulted, the plans can take their views and concerns into account as far as possible. The discussions will often lead to a better solution than council officers and committees can devise on their own and, although the final decision will not necessarily please all of the various parties, they will at least know the issues that needed to be resolved. However, this kind of participation, again, can and often does take place without there being a decentralised council structure.

Fuller proposals in the context of decentralisation to involve people in decisions, not just about their estate or a specific local issue, but about their neighbourhood more broadly, may be worth persevering with but they may, for the reasons given by Gyford and Deakin, ultimately fail to get very far. In the decentralisation context, such 'general' schemes on the part of councils to share powers with residents seem unlikely to make much progress. There may perhaps be a stronger case for separate elected neighbourhood councils or urban parish councils, with specific budgets and limited powers over local matters, as proposed by the Association for Neighbourhood Councils [10].

Scale

An important question is how far the current British concern with decentralisation is, rather as I suggested at the beginning and as Robin Hambleton suggests in his paper, a reaction against the scale of our local authorities, which are much larger and in consequence less accessible than anywhere else in the Western world. Although interest is being shown in decentralisation in other countries as well, the current enthusiasm for it here must to some extent have its origins in the general disenchantment with the 'reform' of local government in the 1960s and 1970s, when much larger scale authorities than previously were created with what is now seen as inadequate evidence. The prospect of yet another upheaval is unwelcome, but it might render less necessary some of the planned decentralisation within authorities. New measures to reverse the earlier errors would need, if at all possible, to command general support among the political parties, though they would raise the difficult and contentious question of two-tier authorities in the metropolitan areas.

Scale is also relevant within decentralising authorities. There is little agreement about what the appropriate scale is. To take the examples of the two local authorities discussed most fully in these papers, the decentralised areas in Birmingham are on average about 12 times larger than an Islington neighbourhood. Decentralisation of housing management alone, with an increase in user control, is probably best done at a lower level still, that of the estate, as with the Priority Estates Project and Safe Neighbourhoods Unit schemes.

Council officers and elected members

Peter Arnold's paper in particular draws attention to the importance to the success of decentralisation of the roles of managers and of professionals such as social workers. Other issues are also raised about the position of council staff and members.

One possible consequence of decentralisation is a shift of control from chief and senior officers to neighbourhood officers and professionals. But it can be argued that the change may actually result in more power for chief officers because they now have more control over the local officers to whom decisions are devolved, thus perhaps weakening the power of elected committees. Another possible effect is to increase the power of the councillor acting for one neighbourhood, relative to that of a committee acting for the whole authority. This might lead to inconsistent results.

Professionals and middle managers, as Peter Arnold shows, are bound to be sensitive to changes in their roles, and their attitudes and behaviour can make a substantial difference to the enthusiasm and effectiveness with which decentralisation is implemented. This can work both ways. Some schemes have apparently been particularly successful because they were welcomed by managers as a better way of doing things. Others have had problems because the proposals were seen as diminishing the powers of managers or the *professional* contribution of professionals.

Staff in all grades can be affected. Office staff in local offices may feel cross-pressured, not certain which voice they should respond to — that of their neighbourhood manager, their departmental line manager or their neighbourhood colleagues from other departments. They may be subject to more pressure from assertive service users, and perhaps from their local councillors, who are likely to have more contact with junior staff through a decentralised structure than they otherwise would. Manual staff may also find that their terms and conditions are changed; in particular their chain of command may be different, and more complex. All these matters have so far been given little or no attention.

Monitoring and evaluation

One of the initial hopes for the seminar was that more would be learned about attempts to monitor and evaluate what is going on. The truth is that, as these papers show, not much can yet be said on the basis of experience to date about how best to proceed in the future.

As noted earlier, we do not seem to have learned much from the earlier decentralisation experiments either. The reason may be, as Nicholas Deakin suggests, that the lessons from that earlier round are deliberately ignored because they have a discouraging story to tell. It seems to me more likely that those who are playing leading parts in the current decentralisation phase know only in vague terms that such schemes were tried but also, and above all, have no knowledge of how successful or unsuccessful they were — mainly because then, as now, there was little serious effort to evaluate what was happening. With local government, as with other social institutions, we seem as a nation to be content to muddle along with new experiments in every generation, learning nothing from past efforts, ever re-inventing a slightly different wheel.

Of course, some useful work is currently being done, for example at the School of Advanced Urban Studies at the University of Bristol, at the Institute of Local Government Studies at the University of Birmingham, at Sheffield City Polytechnic [11], at the Decentralisation Research and Information Centre at the Polytechnic of Central London, and by Howard Elcock and his colleagues at Newcastle-upon-Tyne Polytechnic. This and other work was drawn on at the seminar. But it clearly does not yet amount to much by way of hard evidence of the kind that the researchers themselves would prefer to gather if resources were available.

It has to be acknowledged that there are substantial conceptual and practical difficulties in trying to measure achievement in decentralisation, as with any innovation in institutional form or administrative practice. Such problems can, however, be addressed, as they are in the papers by Hambleton, Cole and Arnold. As Robin Hambleton and Ian Cole point out, a useful contribution has also been made by the National Consumer Council in its *Measuring Up* exercise [12]

The current paucity of evaluation studies, particularly of a rigorous and systematic kind, is certainly a cause for concern. Such assessments of achievement need to be made if politicians and those advising them are to arrive at soundly-based judgements about what is possible and what is not, about the methods that work and those that are less successful, and under what conditions. The seminar confirmed, perhaps more than anything else, the need for more factual evidence on this important development in British local government.

References

[1]   Joseph Rowntree Memorial Trust, *Improving Relations Between Central and Local Government,* Report of a working group, York, Joseph Rowntree Memorial Trust, 1986.

[2]   P. Willmott, *Community in Social Policy,* London, Policy Studies Institute, 1984, p.37.

[3]   Barclay Report, *Social Workers: their Roles and Tasks,* London, Bedford Square Press for National Institute for Social Work, 1982, p.204.

[4]   P. Willmott (editor), *Policing and the Community,* London, Policy Studies Institute, 1987.

[5]   P. Hoggett and R. Hambleton (editors), *Decentralisation and Democracy: localising public services,* Occasional Paper 28, School for Advanced Urban Studies, University of Bristol, 1987.

[6]   P. Arnold and I. Cole, 'The decentralisation of local services: rhetoric and reality' in P. Hoggett and R. Hambleton, ibid.

[7]   Ibid.

[8]   A. Power, *Priority Estates Project 1982. Improving Problem Council Estates: a summary of aims and progress,* London, Department of the Environment, 1982.

[9]   Safe Neighbourhoods Unit, *Confronting Crime: community safety and crime prevention,* London, Safe Neighbourhoods Unit, 1987.

[10] J. Perrin, *Democratically Elected Councils at Neighbourhood Level in Urban Areas,* Birmingham, Association For Neighbourhood Councils, 1986.

[11] The Housing Decentralisation Research Project at Sheffield City is directed by Ian Cole, with Peter Arnold as consultant, and is funded by the Joseph Rowntree Memorial Trust.

[12] National Consumer Council, *Measuring Up. Consumer assessment of local authority services: a guideline study,* London, National Consumer Council, 1986.

2 DEVELOPMENTS, OBJECTIVES AND CRITERIA
Robin Hambleton

Decentralisation is now an extremely popular concept in local government circles. At risk of considerable over-simplification we can contrast two interpretations of the significance of current decentralisation initiatives. On the one hand, a cautious view would assert that we are witnessing an interesting but passing fad. On this analysis the present wave of decentralisation experiments will join their predecessors in oblivion — the neighbourhood offices of the eighties will 'become monuments, like the tower blocks of the sixties and the skateboard parks of the seventies, to a fashion whose time has passed' [1]. On the other hand, it can be argued that there are deep-seated reasons why decentralisation is here to stay. Amongst these we can note that, aided by new information technology, decentralised forms of organisation are rapidly developing within private sector companies across the world and that these managerial innovations are now being imported into the public sector [2]. In addition we know that different forms of decentralisation are proving attractive, in varying degrees, to all the major political parties in Britain and that a large number of local authorities are now committed to a decentralisation strategy of one kind or another.

Later in this paper I argue that analysis of the managerial and political factors involved lends support to the second view — the evidence suggests that decentralisation should now be considered as a significant local government *trend* rather than as a frivolous craze [3]. But, while the *general* direction is clear, there is still much confusion about the precise aims and objectives of decentralisation — in some ways 'decentralisation' is in danger of becoming an empty term because insufficient attention has been given to identifying the specific objectives it is intended to achieve. But first it is essential to place this review in some kind of context by clarifying the scope of the discussion.

Scope of the discussion
This paper focusses on *sub* local authority decentralisation in Britain. It is at this very local level that local government makes an impact (for good or ill) on the communities it is intended to serve [4]. Our first aside should therefore be to note that this is but one level (albeit an important one) within the structure of government. The substantial body of literature which discusses decentralisation in terms of 'the territorial dimension of the state' tells us that

there are *no* totally centralist states in which all governmental authority is concentrated in the headquarters of national government agencies [5]. The choice of central, regional, local and neighbourhood institutions (including the balance of power between these institutions) is one that all governments have to make.

Given the current context of strained central government/local government relations in Britain this reference to higher levels is important. There is now a great deal of evidence to show that the 1980s have witnessed a quite remarkable central government attack on local authority autonomy — this onslaught extends well beyond the battery of fairly familiar financial and legal controls to include a range of more subtle forms of policy control and policy distortion [6]. The broader arguments about the need to strengthen local government vis-a-vis central government are documented elsewhere [7]. And some specific suggestions on how to improve relations between central and local government in the short term have recently been put forward by a Joseph Rowntree Memorial Trust working party [8].

These wider debates about central/local relations are not considered further here, but we should bear them in mind for they have a direct impact on the decentralisation of services to neighbourhood level. Thus, some see decentralisation to neighbourhoods as a means of winning back public support for local government and so bolstering local political opposition to rate-capping and other oppressive Whitehall controls. Others argue that, far from acting as a spur, central government financial constraints have discouraged (if not prevented) the development of decentralisation initiatives in many local authorities.

A second general point is that, though the paper is concerned with experience in Britain, the trend to decentralisation is very much an international phenomenon. A review of developments in Europe has recently been assembled by my colleague Paul Hoggett and in this he notes that radical forms of municipal decentralisation have been pursued far further in Sweden, Italy and elsewhere than in Britain [9]. In addition we should record that decentralisation is seen as a significant tool for development (rather than merely as a form of government organisation) in many Third World countries [10].

A third point, touched upon by Bob Davies in his paper on voluntary and community groups, is that, whilst decentralisation is usually concerned with shifting power and influence to a number of smaller *geographical* units (areas, neighbourhoods or whatever), it is also possible to talk of decentralising local government by strengthening and expanding the non-statutory sector, that is by decentralising influence to *groups* rather than areas [11]. Nicholas Deakin has rightly observed that the neighbourhood, however defined, does not necessarily command its inhabitants' primary loyalties:

As citizens, most people have a variety of cross-cutting allegiances, some to locality, some explicitly to neighbours or friends, some to relations, some to peer groups, some to ethnic or gender groupings, others deriving from occupation or work place. These allegiances co-exist and assume different levels of importance at different times [12].

The idea of decentralising influence to groups overlaps with decentralisation to areas because many area-based initiatives place a strong emphasis on stimulating and supporting the voluntary sector.

Finally, we should note that this paper embraces both the decentralisation and the democratisation of public services. These two parallel but distinct approaches to the reform of the welfare state are discussed later in the paper. At this point, however, we can affirm that fruitful discussion of 'local government decentralisation and community' cannot be limited to an agenda which views local government purely as an *administrative* system. Administrative arrangements *are* important — it can be argued that decentralised management is essential to enhance the responsiveness of service providers to service consumers. However, discussion of ways of improving the relationship between the town hall and the public it serves needs to go beyond consumerist models and recognise that local government is both an administrative and a *political* system. Many of the current decentralisation initiatives seek to promote a new style of politics which empowers groups and interests previously on the margins of local authority decision making structures [13]. In one sense then the trend to decentralisation can be viewed as a search for 'new forms of democracy' which seek to alter liberal or representative democracy by either increasing the scope or transforming the methods of democratic decision making [14]. This theme is explored further by John Gyford in his paper discussing the impact of decentralisation on democracy.

The development of decentralisation
This section provides a brief chronological overview of developments relating to decentralisation in the last 15 years or so. First a quote:

> Perhaps most important ... these geographical sub-committees will have direct contact with community groups, neighbourhood councils and other voluntary organisations in their respective areas. They are currently engaged in identifying and getting acquainted with community groups and voluntary bodies in their areas, and talking with the council's officers about existing programmes and problems [15].

Interestingly, this is *not* the latest update on developments in a radical London borough — this is the Town Clerk of Stockport writing in 1971. Whilst there are important differences between the area management initiatives of the 1970s and decentralisation in the 1980s, there are also important connections which are often ignored in current debates. Much can be gained from studying the experiences of the 1970s — not just in terms of area management but also in relation to participation and community development.

Let us start with *area management*. Stockport was the first authority in Britain to experiment with an area committee system designed to move towards a corporate approach at the local level, and it was the first to introduce a formal area organisation into its management structure at both the member and the officer level in 1974. As a corporate planner working for the Chief Executive I was heavily involved in the development of Stockport's area management system in the mid-1970s. We had area co-ordinators, area committees, local information officers, a strong emphasis on community development and we even attempted to build community views directly into the council's policy making and resource allocating machinery [16]. The Department of the Environment took an interest in these innovations which chimed in with ideas emerging from the Department's own research on urban management [17]. A series of 'area management trials' was launched and by 1977-78 various reports appeared outlining the potential of area management for tackling departmentalism and improving service responsiveness [18]. My own research at the time examined the development of neighbourhood policies in Britain and the United States and provided an international comparison of area management in five innovating cities [19]. The main conclusion that can be drawn from the area management initiatives of the 1970s is that, whilst a wide range of specific (and mainly modest) improvements in local government effectiveness can be identified, the lasting outcome is that, despite high aspirations, the practice of local authority management and the nature of local political activity remained substantially unchanged.

If we now turn to *public participation and community development* we can record the growth of a remarkably wide range of innovations in the period from 1968 [20]. Gyford interprets these as a major shift from the idea of viewing local authorities simply as guardians of the common good towards an approach in which authorities accord greater recognition to *sectional interests* [21]. Thus, we now have a variety of consultation arrangements (some enshrined in legislation) relating to, for example, town planning, education, housing, social services, leisure and the arts, commerce, ethnic minorities and women's issues. In the early 1970s there was a swift expansion of community work in Britain which was seen as a new and rapidly growing activity in its own right. A key book on community work enthused: 'new ideas and approaches are being generated ... much faster than the rate at which they are being written down, digested and analysed' [22]. It was a heady time.

For a variety of reasons the late 1970s witnessed a retreat from the ambitions of the late 1960s and the early 1970s. The 'participatory democracy' which some believed to be just around the corner did not materialise. The reasons are complex, but we can point to two key features. First, the work of many of the 12 Home Office funded Community Development Projects pointed to the limitations of localised community development strategies when not coupled with wider policy changes to combat inequality [23]. Second, public expenditure restraint from 1974-75 (following on from the oil/economic crisis of 1973-74) reduced the funds available for innovation and many local authority departments became inward looking and cautious. The 'urban' professions were able to reassert their resistance to both 'political' control and public 'participation' in decision making [24]. Arguably the most significant link from the community initiatives of the early 1970s to the decentralisation movement of the 1980s is that many community activists later became local authority councillors and brought into the council chamber considerable hostility towards the conventional workings of local authorities [25].

A key turning point, and a source of inspiration for many of the politically motivated decentralisation initiatives of recent years, was the election of a Labour council in Walsall in May 1980. The underlying philosophy of their manifesto was that 'socialism is most likely to be achieved in this country through participative democracy' [26]. Decentralisation, they argued, would break down the remoteness of local government, spread knowledge of how the system can be controlled locally, and increase people's experience and confidence to participate and make decisions. By the time they lost control two years later the council had established 32 neighbourhood offices offering a comprehensive housing service covering both public and private sectors [27]. The officers also provide welfare rights advice, organise domiciliary care services and undertake community work. After the Labour Party lost control to a Conservative-Alliance coalition in May 1982, there were moves to close some of the neighbourhood offices. However, the offices had already shown that they provided a beneficial service in Conservative areas as well as Labour areas and only two were closed [28].

Walsall became the 'unlikely location for the New Jerusalem' and 'coachloads of eager seekers after truth' visited the town in the early 1980s [29]. The May 1982 London local government elections saw decentralisation feature boldly in many London Labour Party manifestos — including Islington, Camden, Hackney and Lewisham. In recent years a growing number of other Labour authorities have followed suit including major cities like Birmingham, Manchester, Edinburgh, Glasgow and Leeds as well as smaller towns like Basildon, Harlow and Reading. The London borough of Islington leads the way nationally having now opened all of its 24 multi-service neighbourhood offices and begun to create neighbourhood forums composed of local people which will influence service provision and local spending [30]. Liz du Parcq outlines the Islington experience in her paper.

However, it would be wrong to see decentralisation as the political property of the Labour left. Since May 1986 the Liberal controlled borough of Tower Hamlets has moved swiftly to introduce a system of neighbourhood committees and neighbourhood offices [31]. Conservative controlled Cambridgeshire County Council has gone further than any local authority in developing decentralised, school based budgeting and financial management [32]. And decentralised forms of working are now being advocated for certain parts of the health service [33]. Meanwhile, decentralisation enjoys considerable professional support in some local authority departments as a means of improving service management. Thus in social services there have been innovations in, for example, East Sussex, Humberside and elsewhere [34]. And there are widespread moves to decentralise housing management — the London Borough of Newham provides a particularly interesting example because a lot of attention is being given to staff training and staff development [35]. However, some of these professionally led forms of decentralisation have been strongly criticised by those keen to improve people's say and involvement in services [36]. With the space available it is impossible to offer much comment on these various decentralisation initiatives. Other sources are available which provide reports on the problems as well as the successes [37]. Instead I would now like to outline a simple conceptual map which has proved useful in a number of seminars and workshops Paul Hoggett and I have run on various aspects of decentralisation and 'getting closer to the consumer' in the last year or so.

A conceptual map
Our map contrasts 'old solutions' (broadly pre-1980) with the 'new patterns' of the 1980s [38]. The phrase *bureaucratic pluralism* succinctly describes the old solutions which have become today's problems in local government. The last five years have not only seen a crisis in these old solutions, but the emergence of two major alternatives. The first alternative, usually associated with the radical right, seeks to challenge the very notion of collective and non-market provision for public need. Centring upon the strategy of *privatisation* it seeks to replace public provision with private provision. The second emerging alternative aims to preserve the notion of public provision, but seeks a *radical reform* of the manner in which this provision in undertaken. Thus it seeks to replace the old bureaucratic paternalist model with a much more responsive and democratic model. This latter approach to reform appears to have two central variants the one being essentially *consumerist,* the other being essentially *collectivist.* The old and new solutions are schematically outlined in Figure 1. Having provided an overall map we can now sketch in a few details.

There are two developing critiques of the old solutions. First, there is the *political* critique of massive alienating public bureaucracies. This analysis suggests that the Thatcher government has cashed in on the paternalism and inadequacies of the welfare state and that the response must be radical. David Blunkett, for example, takes this view:

> We must start debating as a movement our values and the ways in which we will extend democracy, participative democracy, as well as defending what we've got; because it is partly the inadequacy of, and the alienation from, the way in which the system is worked that has enabled Thatcher to take the steps she has with such success [39].

Second, there is the *management* critique of inward looking organisational cultures — the widespread failure in the private as well as the public sector to put the 'customer' first. The critique has been developed in popular form by Peters and Waterman in their book *In Search of Excellence* [40]. On the basis of their research they identified eight criteria which characterised the 'excellent' companies. Inter alia, these companies:
have a bias for action;
recognise that employees are the source of quality and productivity;
have a clear basic philosophy (almost an ideology); and
listen intently and regularly to the customer.
The point I wish to stress here is that both the political and the managerial critiques suggest that radical rather than marginal change is needed.

Figure 1:
Emerging patterns of relationship between local authorities and their
communities: a conceptual map

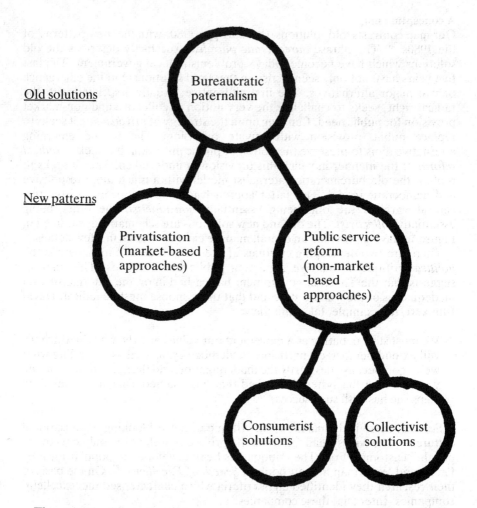

The *privatisation* option takes several forms ranging from selling off assets
(for example council house sales) through rights to private substitution (for
example the right to repair) to contracting out services to the private sector (for
example refuse collection). From the point of view of this discussion the
contracting out of public services to the private sector is potentially the most
significant. Supporters of this approach believe that private contractors can
often provide a more efficient service due to the nature of competition within
the commercial sector and superior resource management. Opponents argue
that contracting out leads to a less effective service as a result of short-term

profit considerations and the incentive to cut costs.

The major alternative to privatisation is public service reform. This approach recognises that a successful defence of the welfare state requires a response which goes well beyond defending existing forms of service provision to develop new ways forward which will win popular support. The map distinguishes two kinds of public service reform The first, which is essentially *consumerist* in its orientation, gives primary emphasis to enhancing the responsiveness of local government services [41]. The second, which we have labelled *collectivist,* gives primary emphasis to the *democratisation* of local government service provision. Clearly there are very close links between the responsiveness and the democracy of public services. Nevertheless it is quite possible to distinguish between local authorities (such as Walsall and East Sussex) whose primary concern has been to make local government more responsive but who have made few efforts to tackle the problem of who controls the planning and delivery of services, and local authorities (such as Islington) where the question of public control has been placed much more firmly on the agenda alongside concerns relating to responsiveness.

Clearly both the emerging consumerist and collectivist solutions require fundamental changes in terms of the relationship between local authorities and the communities that they serve. However, as suggested earlier, the consumerist approach is essentially concerned with the reform of local government considered as an *administrative system,* whereas the collectivist approach essentially seeks to reform local government considered as a *political* system.

It is important to recognise that there is a tension between these two approaches. In a sense, Walsall's very success has proved part of its failure. Precisely because it has created a set of very responsive local government services (through the creation of 32 neighbourhood offices) demand has increased enormously. As a consequence the decentralised staff find that they are responding to the community in a very reactive and individualistic fashion and wider objectives concerned with community development have had to be set aside. Equally one can see how attempts to develop new forms of local accountability within local government may divert energy and resources away from the more routine, but no less important, task of providing an efficient and responsive service.

Objectives — consumerism or collectivism or both?
We think it would be a mistake for those concerned with decentralisation to divide into two incommunicative camps — the 'consumerists' and the 'collectivists'. Advance in both areas are needed. At present a great deal of useful innovation is taking place within the consumerist perspective. Apart from the decentralising local authorities (opening accessible neighbourhood offices, etc.) many other authorities are experimenting with ways of 'getting closer to the consumer' — ranging from survey research on public opinions, through positive marketing of services, to new ways of getting customer feedback (for example freephones). Those concerned to emphasise the democratisation of public services should not dismiss these developments

merely because they have a private sector ring.

At the same time there are significant limitations to the consumerist approach mainly because it fails to address the issue of power. There are two main reasons why it is necessary to go beyond the consumerist approach in local government and empower the consumer.

The first stems from the need to recognise that many of these consumerist ideas have been imported from the private sector where, within limits, the consumer enjoys a degree of power by virtue of personal choice. If a retailer in the 'market place' is too expensive or sells a shoddy product it is possible (for most of us) to shop elsewhere. If a council tenant is receiving a poor service it is extremely difficult, if not impossible, to switch landlords. The contrast then is between the shopper who has some power (often a great deal) in the server/ served relationship and the local authority service user who is virtually powerless. We would argue that it is this imbalance of power in the server/ served relationship which accounts for many of the drawbacks with current forms of service provision by the welfare state. The consumerist approach fails to address this imbalance of power or the absence of choice within the public sector.

The second major limitation of the consumerist approach is that it has difficulty coping with the needs of *groups* of consumers. Unlike private companies local authorities have both 'individual' and 'collective' consumers and there are therefore clear limits to an individual approach. Clean air, roads, environmental quality, footpaths, street lighting, and schooling are just some of the services that are both provided and consumed on a collective basis.

Perhaps a more specific example will illustrate our point. A local authority housing department certainly needs to be able to develop ways of responding swiftly and sensitively to the needs of individual tenants, but the department will also need to develop new ways of relating to the collective tenant. Many local authority housing decisions (for example concerning local environment improvements or play facilities or meeting room facilities or lighting systems for external areas on an estate) seek to address collective problems or needs that tenants may have. There are likely to be conflicts of view within the community on how best to tackle these issues and, in a healthy democracy, these views need to be given expression and need to be heard. More than that, people need to be able to influence decisions if they are not to become alienated and distrustful.

So far we have pointed to the limitations of the consumerist approach even within a frame of reference concerned mainly with service responsiveness. However, if the frame is broadened to embrace wider objectives related to strengthening local democracy (as a contribution to sustaining democracy as a whole) and diffusing power and responsibility within society then the limitations of a consumerist approach become ever more visible. Hence the attraction of what we have called collectivist solutions. Such solutions need a renewed emphasis on community development [42].

So far this discussion of objectives has been couched in broad terms. It is possible to be more specific and identify five overlapping yet distinct objectives — see Figure 2 [43]. Some of these are clearly more closely identified with a consumerist approach — for example, improving services. Others are more

Figure 2:
Objectives of decentralisation

1. Improving services

    — Service delivery (convenient, integrated, one-stop)

    — Service planning and policy

    — The relationship between public servants and the public — public at the top

2. Local accountability

    — Vary degrees — authority or influence?

    — To whom? (Local councillors? Community groups? Local people? A combination?)

    — Community development

3. Distribution

    — Different resources for different areas/groups

    — Equal opportunities policy

4. Political awareness

    — Win political support for public services

    — Win support for a political party

5. Staffing

    — Job satisfaction

    — Multi-disciplinary teams

    — Friendly environment

    — Neighbourhood loyalty

obviously collectivist — for example, strengthening local accountability. Whilst many of these objectives are reinforcing it is important to recognise that some are in tension if not conflict. Thus a radical approach to strengthening accountability of services to the neighbourhood (in line with the second objective) could be incompatible with the pursuit of authority wide policies concerned to even up opportunities for neglected groups (the third objective). The staffing objectives can be regarded as ends in themselves (in the sense of improving the experience of work for state employees) but can also be regarded as essential first steps to achieving other objectives. The potential of decentralisation for staff development is considerable and is beginning to be recognised in some authorities [44].

Measuring success and failure

How do we measure the success or failure of decentralisation initiatives? Answer: it all depends on what you want to achieve, and who *you* are anyway. This may seem a peculiarly evasive reply, but we must recognise that the different actors will have different meanings of success. Thus it should not surprise us if the leader of a local council has a different approach to measuring the success of decentralisation from, say, a member of a local community group. This recognition draws us close to some of the fundamentals underlying social scientific inquiry:

> Information and data can never be understood in isolation from the context of ideas which give them meaning. And it is these frames, or modes, or values, or ideologies, or theories, or whatever we choose to call them, which are crucial for any creative work; for without them we have no question to ask. Problem-setting is as important as problem-solving because the frames which organise thoughts shape the conclusions we reach [45].

There has been a dearth of evaluative work on decentralisation. It is not difficult to see why this should be so. Practitioners will have lots of good arguments about the extraordinary work demands arising from developing a decentralised organisation. 'It is quite enough to get decentralisation to happen without at the same time trying to crawl over everything we do to see if it's working perfectly' is an understandable response. Meanwhile academics and other researchers have not (on the whole) demonstrated that they have an understanding of the dynamics of organisational change and the nature of local political struggles relating to decentralisation — still less have they shown that they can provide evaluation frameworks which are inventive enough to work helpfully in practice. In any event there may, in some authorities, be a strong resistance to the very idea of any form of evaluation which is separate from the electoral process. On this model the argument runs: 'If the electorate don't like decentralisation they will change the party in control; if they do like it the party will be returned. Who needs evaluation when we have local democracy?'

In my view these arguments against evaluation do not stand up very well. If one accepts the position, argued earlier in this paper, that decentralisation is a significant local government trend then the widespread failure to embark on fairly extensive evaluation of these initiatives is indefensible. There are several dimensions which deserve more study. For example, Peter Arnold and Ian Cole argue for research on three themes: (i) resistance to decentralisation (since there has been a lot); (ii) the relationship between decentralisation and management control; and (iii) continuous monitoring and appraisal of progress with decentralisation [46]. Readers will have their own priorities. Whatever the focus for evaluation it may be helpful to distinguish two broad approaches. Each has strengths and limitations and they are not mutually exclusive.

First, there are important evaluation issues relating to 'hard' quantitative data about the effectiveness of service provision. Take, for example, response times in dealing with requests for housing repairs — have they gone up or have they gone down? With evaluation questions of this kind we soon enter the world of performance indicators and so called 'value for money' studies so loved by management consultants and the Audit Commission [47]. Such indicators and cost appraisals are being used increasingly in the health service and elsewhere in the public sector. Some commentators now argue that quantitative, performance measurement of this kind can be counter-productive. For them to work performance measures need to be integrated with the management process and culture of an organisation. If this is not the case 'they will become no more than a mildly irritating exercise in the collection of statistics' [48].

It is also true that such indicators need careful interpretation. For example, when area repair teams began operating out of neighbourhood offices in Islington the waiting time for repairs was immediately reduced dramatically. However, once tenants heard about the improvement in service more repair requests were made with the result that, in many areas of the borough, waiting times have increased (although they have not gone back up to pre-decentralisation levels). From the point of view of an individual tenant waiting for a repair the service might be experienced as being little different despite the fact that truly remarkable increases in overall productivity have been achieved. Having made these cautionary remarks about performance indicators it has to be said that most local authorities are failing to ask quite basic questions about the impact of decentralisation — about the additional level of demand caused by localising services, about service productivity and about costs.

The second broad approach to evaluation is illustrated by a recent and excellent study of local authority service performance by the National Consumer Council [49]. This provides a useful framework for moving beyond the 'hard' data approach of performance indicators to embrace issues relating to the 'soft' data of consumer experience. This approach, which was tested out across a wide range of services in a couple of local authorities, set out (i) to encourage local authorities to set explicit targets for their 'consumer performance' and to evaluate and report on their achievements and (ii) to provide local government consumers with information which will enable them to raise questions about the performance of their authorities. Some of the recommended indicators are quantifiable, others are non-quantifiable.

My own view is that it is particularly important to combine study of the outcomes of decentralisation with analysis of the process of decentralisation.

Unless we do this we will not be well placed to explain why policies have been successes or failures [50]. As part of such an approach it would be possible to draw lessons from recent research work which has taken the form of a kind of pluralistic evaluation — an approach which takes more account of the different perceptions of success different interest groups will have. A recent study of a day hospital is suggestive [51] This identified several 'meanings of success' including: free patient flow, clinical cure for patients, provision of an integrated service, beneficial impact in related services, support for relatives, service of high quality. A pluralistic evaluation of, say, a neighbourhood office would not only bring into the open these different 'meanings of success' — it would also facilitate exploration of the quality of services including the quality of the relationships between the local authority and the people it is intended to serve.

Conclusion

This paper has ranged fairly broadly over a number of issues relating to decentralisation. My intention has been to provide an overview of some of the main issues relating to 'local government decentralisation and community' which can provide a context for the more specific papers which follow. The theme which I would like to close with is the theme of learning. We could be doing much more to facilitate learning from past experience (with area management, public involvement, etc.) and from current experience (both within and between different local authority areas).

References

1   N. Deakin, 'The fashionable choice', *Community Care*, 18 April 1985, pp.12-14.

2   P. Hoggett, 'A long wave to freedom', *Chartist*, October/November 1985, pp.25-8; T.J. Peters and R.H. Waterman, *In Search of Excellence. Lessons from America's best-run companies,* New York, Harper and Row, 1982.

3   This evidence is set out in some detail in a new book: P. Hoggett and R. Hambleton (editors), *Decentralisation and Democracy: localising public services,* Occasional Paper 28, School for Advanced Urban Studies, University of Bristol, 1987.

4   I say 'communities' rather than 'community' to emphasise the diversity of interest groups and interests found in any local authority area.

5   B.C. Smith, *Decentralisation: the territorial dimension of the state,* London, George Allen and Unwin, 1985, p.1.

6   R. Hambleton, *Rethinking Policy Planning. A study of planning systems linking central and local government,* School for Advanced Urban Studies, University of Bristol, 1986, Chapters 2 and 3.

7   G. Jones and J. Stewart, *The Case for Local Government*, London, George Allen and Unwin, 1983.

8   Joseph Rowntree Memorial Trust, *Improving Relations Between Central and Local Government*, Report of a working group, York, Joseph Rowntree Memorial Trust, 1986.

9   P. Hoggett, 'Political parties, community action and the reform of municipal government in Europe' in Hoggett and Hambleton, op.cit, Chapter 3.

10   D. Conyers, 'Decentralisation and development: a review of the literature', *Public Administration and Development*, 4, 1984, pp.187-197; see also the special issue on decentralisation and local control of the *Community Development Journal*, 21(2).

11   This notion of 'welfare pluralism' is touched on in R. Hambleton and P. Hoggett (editors), *The Politics of Decentralisation: theory and practice of a radical local government initiative*, Working Paper 46, School for Advanced Urban Studies, University of Bristol, 1984, p.2.

12   N. Deakin 'Decentralisation: panacea or blind alley', *Local Government Policy Making*, July 1984, p.20.

13   K. Beuret and G. Stoker, 'The Labour Party and neighbourhood decentralisation: flirtation or commitment?', *Critical Social Policy*, 17; G. Stoker, 'Labour and local government: breaking the statist mould in welfare service delivery', *Social Policy and Administration*, 21(1).

14   D. Held and C. Pollitt, *New Forms of Democracy*, London, Open University/Sage, 1986. (These ideas overlap with discussions about the democratisation of economic activity involving a shift from commodity production to socially useful production. See S. Bodington, M. George and J. Michaelson, *Developing the Socially Useful Economy*, London, Macmillan, 1986, pp.189-98.)

15   D.W. Hay, 'Division organisation in Stockport', *Local Government Chronicle*, 24 July 1971, p.1318.

16   R. Hambleton, 'Preferences for policies', *Municipal Journal*, 25 July 1975, pp.979-83.

17   Department of the Environment, *Making Towns Better. Reports on Sunderland, Rotherham and Oldham*, London, HMSO, 1973; Department of the Environment, *Proposals for Area Management. Liverpool inner area study*, November 1973.

[18]   A. Davis et al, *The Management of Deprivation. Final report of Southwark community development project,* Polytechnic of the South Bank, 1977; K.J. Harrop et al, *The Implementation and Development of Area Management,* Institute of Local Government Studies, University of Birmingham, 1978.

[19]   R. Hambleton, *Policy Planning and Local Government,* London, Hutchinson, 1978.

[20]   N. Boaden et al, *Public Participation in Local Services,* London, Longman, 1982.

[21]   J. Gyford, 'Diversity, sectionalism and local democracy' in *Aspects of Local Democracy,* Research Volume IV of *The (Widdicombe) Inquiry into the Conduct of Local Authority Business,* London, HMSO, 1986.

[22]   D. Jones and M. Mayo (editors), *Community Work One,* London, Routledge and Kegan Paul, 1974, p.xiii.

[23]   There is a vast literature here. A useful guide is provided by M. Loney, *Community Against Government. The British community development project 1968-78,* London, Heinemann, 1983.

[24]   P. Dunleavy, *Urban Political Analysis,* London, Macmillan, 1980, pp.112-9.

[25]   J. Gyford, *The Politics of Local Socialism,* London, George Allen and Unwin, 1985, Chapters 2 and 3.

[26]   *Walsall's haul to democracy — the neighbourhood concept,* Walsall Labour Party Manifesto, May 1980.

[27]   C. Fudge, 'Decentralisation: socialism goes local?' in M. Boddy and C. Fudge (editors), *Local Socialism? Labour councils and new left alternatives,* London, Macmillan, 1984, pp.195-8.

[28]   J. Seabrook, *The Idea of Neighbourhood,* London, Pluto, 1984, p.127. Since then another office has opened so that there are now 31. In May 1986 Labour regained control of the council and new proposals establishing eight 'across-the-board' local committees were approved before Christmas and will begin operation in March/April 1987.

[29]   N. Deakin, 'Two cheers for decentralisation' in A. Wright, et al, *Socialism and Decentralisation,* Tract 496, London, Fabian Society, 1984.

[30]   London Borough of Islington, *Going Local. Decentralisation in practice,* London, Islington Council Press, 1986.

31 J. Morphet, 'Local authority decentralisation — Tower Hamlets goes all the way', *Policy and Politics*, 15(2), pp.119-126.

32 T. Burgess, 'Cambridgeshire's financial management initiative for schools', *Public Money*, June 1986, pp.21-4.

33 Community Nursing Review Team (Chair Julia Cumberlege), *Neighbourhood Nursing — a focus for care*, London, HMSO, 1986; Department of Health and Social Security, *Primary Health Care — an agenda for discussion*, London, HMSO, 1986. Locality (or area based) planning of health services is developing in some district health authorities, for example, Exeter.

34 H. Elcock, 'Decentralisation as a tool for social services management', *Local Government Studies*, July/August 1986, pp.35-49; S. Hatch (editor), *Decentralisation and Care in the Community*, London, Policy Studies Institute, 1985.

35 A. Rivers, 'Training for change in Newham's housing service' in Hoggett and Hambleton, op.cit, Chapter 9; see also A. Power, *Local Housing Management. A priority estates project survey*, London, Department of the Environment, 1984.

36 P. Beresford and S. Croft, *Whose Welfare? Private care or public services*, Lewis Cohen Urban Studies Centre, Brighton Polytechnic, 1986; F. Winkler, 'Consumerism in health care: beyond the supermarket model', *Policy and Politics*, 15(1), pp.1-8; S. Adamson and S. Wilson, *Tenant Participation*, Paper to the *Going Local — devolving power* conference organised by the Decentralisation Research and Information Centre, Polytechnic of Central London, 5 February 1987.

37 Hoggett and Hambleton, op.cit.; see also *Going Local* newsletter produced on a quarterly basis by the Decentralisation Research and Information Centre, Polytechnic of Central London.

38 A fuller exposition of this map appears in R. Hambleton and P. Hoggett, 'Beyond bureaucratic paternalism' in Hoggett and Hambleton, op.cit., Chapter 1.

39 D. Blunkett, 'Ratecap resistance', *Marxism Today*, March 1985, p.9.

40 Peters and Waterman, op.cit.

41 Paul Hoggett and I have benefitted from exchanges with John Stewart and Michael Clarke in developing these ideas. Their paper on the 'public service orientation' makes some important general points about public service as a key value and about the management consequences of

adopting such an approach. See M. Clarke and J. Stewart, 'Local government and the public service orientation' *Local Government Studies,* 12(3).

[42] J. Smith and G. Chanan, 'Public service and community development', *Local Government Studies,* 13(1), pp.7-14.

[43] These are set out more fully in Hambleton and Hoggett (editors), op.cit., pp.5-9.

[44] There is a wider range of issues here relating to the industrial relations aspect of decentralisation which local authorities neglect at their peril. See E. Heery, 'A common labour movement? Left Labour councils and trade unions' in Hoggett and Hambleton op.cit., Chapter 11.

[45] M. Rein, *Social Science and Public Policy,* Harmondworth, Penguin, 1976, p.14.

[46] P. Arnold and I. Cole, 'The decentralisation of local services: rhetoric and reality' in Hoggett and Hambleton, op.cit., Chapter 7.

[47] For example, Audit Commission, *Managing the Crisis in Council Housing,* London, HMSO, 1986.

[48] N. Flynn, 'Performance measurement in public sector services', *Policy and Politics,* 14(3), pp.389-404.

[49] National Consumer Council, *Measuring Up. Consumer assessment of local authority services: a guideline study,* London, National Consumer Council, 1986.

[50] H. Wolman, 'The determinants of programme success and programme failure', *Journal of Public Policy,* 1(4), pp.433-64.

[51] G. Smith and C. Cantley, *Assessing Health Care. A study in organisational evaluation,* Open University Press, 1985.

3 NEIGHBOURHOOD SERVICES: THE ISLINGTON EXPERIENCE

Liz du Parcq

By the early 1980s inner London borough councils were beginning to put a high priority on improving the quality of local government services. There was a need to counter feelings of alienation in the community and to tackle issues of political credibility associated with the measurable decline in service quality, symptoms of which included high levels of empty council homes, rapidly rising rent arrears, increasing levels of homelessness, an intractable squatting problem, and slowness and inefficiency in dealing with housing repairs. Public and councillors alike were frustrated by problems of departmentalism and division of responsibility between separate parts of big council departments. There were very strong messages to councillors from the community which boiled down to feelings of powerlessness in the face of an apparently uncaring bureaucracy the structures of which were geared to the convenience and economy of the service providers rather than the needs of the consumers.

Several London authorities emerged from the 1982 council elections with a commitment to follow the lead of Walsall and decentralise services to neighbourhood level. Islington's priority was to open neighbourhood offices and locate all the principal personal service providers in them during the lifetime of the 1982-86 administration. This was seen to be an important first stage in what had to be an irreversible process. Devolution of power to the local communities in the neighbourhoods would follow. Islington's neighbourhood approach has been by far the most comprehensive to get off the ground in London so far. The planned 24 neighbourhood offices were all open by March 1987; some of them had been in operation for two years. This is therefore an opportune time for a first appraisal of the success of Islington's neighbourhood approach in improving the quality of local government service provision. Islington Council itself is drawing upon its experience to formulate a strategy for the next three years, a strategy which includes as one of its principal elements: 'Making decentralisation really work'.

The aims of Islington's approach to decentralisation were to improve accessibility to services, to coordinate the delivery of the different services and to devolve power to the local community to control the delivery of those services. Accessibility was to be achieved not just by locating neighbourhood offices in the focal points of 24 neighbourhoods where people could walk to them easily but by making them accessible to people with disabilities, and open plan with no physical barriers to separate staff and users. Furthermore the style was to be one of openness and service-orientation and the staff were to be recruited in such a way as to reflect the ethnic make-up of the local community and to provide where possible speakers of all the borough's minority languages. The accessibility objective has to a large extent already been achieved.

Achievement of effective coordination of services at neighbourhood level is a gradual process involving more than just locating staff from the old housing districts and social services teams in the same neighbourhood office and providing some generic administrative support. Significant benefits have undoubtedly been achieved through simple co-location of service providers. Their styles still tend to be dictated by departmental and service committee priorities but, despite the limitations imposed by the existing committee structures and management styles, staff in the offices have progressed from talking to each other face to face for the first time to some innovative and exciting new approaches to service delivery. Environmental health and housing officers now cooperate in dealing with private sector improvements; housing management and benefit staff liaise with welfare rights workers and social workers in arrears chasing, debt counselling and take-up campaigns. It is estimated that in 1986 welfare rights officers helped to secure £½m in DHSS single payments for Islington residents. Real inter-departmental coordination in the way the needs of the neighbourhood are evaluated and subsequently met has yet to become a reality but there are encouraging signs that staff in the offices are moving towards more generic ways of working and more imaginative use of staff resources — in spite sometimes of the central bureaucracy, the central leadership of the council's trade unions and the central political pressures.

Setting up and staffing 24 neighbourhood offices was an enormous organisational undertaking but politically it was the easy part. Much more difficult has been democratising the process, giving power back to the community and enabling local people to set the service priorities and become genuinely involved in the resource allocation process. There are three main constraints to effective delegation and devolution of power — the unwillingness of those who have the power to part with any of it, the less than enthusiastic response from the neighbourhood/community to the particular brand of democratisation actually on offer and the inertia of the local government system, particularly in a time of dwindling resources.

Impact on services
In the relatively short time Islington's neighbourhood offices have been open, there has already been a significant impact on services and on the level of public demand for them. Prior to decentralisation, the direct labour organisation handled 1,500 repairs a week, with an average backlog of 10 to 13 weeks. By the end of 1986, not only had the average response time been reduced to under three weeks but the number of repairs completed by the area repair teams and the residual central trades had doubled to nearly 3,000 a week. Tenants are making more requests for repairs and thereby demonstrating much greater

faith in the system, but delays are still greater than tenants had been led to expect they would be in the pre-decentralisation political build-up. Because decentralisation has failed to deliver on the entirety of people's increased expectations, there are still complaints from, for example, tenants' leaders about performance on repairs.

There have been measurable improvements across the whole range of housing services — rent arrears had stopped increasing by the summer of 1986 and housing benefits backlogs are a thing of the past. Demand for social services has exceeded expectations, particularly in neighbourhoods which were previously some distance from an area team. There has not as yet however been any systematic research done on measuring the impact on consumer satisfaction levels. Several academic institutions have expressed an interest in helping with this work and I hope we shall get some research under way during the coming year. Anecdotal evidence suggests increased consumer satisfaction, and that generally people like the offices and trust the staff. But this trust can very easily turn to resentment if an estate manager is not available when the tenant calls, if a computer system error leads to incorrect rent arrears showing on a rent card, if the telephone is not answered quickly or if an office closes due to staff shortages or a failed heating system. We are still unfortunately plagued by relatively minor industrial disputes about gradings and job descriptions which inevitably impinge on the service to the public.

There was a deliberate build-up of client expectations before decentralisation as part of the political process of convincing everyone inside and outside the council that it was going to happen and that the substantial investment involved would pay off in improved service delivery. But however much service quality improves, however available and charming our gatekeepers become, decentralisation does not have an answer for the fundamental inadequacy of resources to deal with inner London's escalating problems of poverty, deprivation and homelessness. In 1982, when Islington started work on decentralising its services, there were no Islington families in bed and breakfast accommodation. Now there are 125. The number of families waiting for a better place to live has increased. In the neighbourhood office a tenant can see on a computer screen that his or her transfer application is correctly prioritised (and that is a significant improvement in itself) but that can only be a small consolation for the delay in obtaining a transfer, because of the widening gap between needs and resources in inner London.

We know that services are more available and better coordinated and that this is paying off in particular areas — notably reducing the numbers of empty properties, speeding up repairs and tackling the worst symptoms of poverty. We also know that our workforce is more representative of the community it serves and that we are beginning to reach the minority ethnic groups in the borough and give them and all other under-represented sections of the community better access to council services and to the decision-making structures of the council. The moves towards greater genericism in service delivery and a more open approach are not however universally welcomed — the relatively powerful tenants' lobby has for example complained about the presence of certain types of social services clients in the offices in a way which suggests that they would very much rather such people used a different entrance. Sometimes there is aggressive behaviour in the neighbourhood offices, occasionally violence, but we remain convinced that the better relationships which generally exist between staff and public are a direct result of removing all barricades and security screens from the contact points between staff and the public (except of course for cash collection points).

Power

I turn now to the second, and more politically difficult, phase of Islington's decentralisation process — the devolution of power to neighbourhood level. The commitment to decentralisation contained a promise of local democracy and transfer of decision-making on a range of issues to neighbourhood forums. Six of the 24 are now formally constituted though their powers remain advisory only and limited in extent. They advise neighbourhood officers on how to spend neighbourhood allocations for environmental improvements and a small revenue 'community budget'. For most purposes the forums and the as yet embryonic steering groups can only act in an advisory capacity, reacting to consultation when it happens, exerting pressure for policy changes, and making bids on the dwindling and increasingly 'committed' capital programme.

Interest from the community in forums is real but as yet limited in extent. For some sections of the community — notably the disabled, minority ethnic groups, the elderly, the young, and many women — neighbourhood forums offer the first real chance of influencing the way council services are delivered. But they are cautious and in some cases suspicious about the extent of the power being offered. One large interest group, the traditional tenants' associations, see the neighbourhood forums, which will involve all sections of the community, as potentially 'watering down' the special relationship which they have enjoyed as tenants with the council as their landlords over the last 15 years or so — a relationship which has involved representation on council committees and their own network of district committees. The extent of the threat which tenants' leaders perceive neighbourhood forums to be can be gauged by their success in ensuring the preservation of a parallel system of district tenants' forums and the tactics which some of them are currently employing to delay formal constitution of neighbourhood forums until they have managed to secure undertakings that all matters relating in any way to 'housing' are decided in special housing sub-groups of the neighbourhood forums composed only of tenants' association representatives.

Much more fundamental however to the success of Islington's neighbourhood strategy is the extent to which the 'centre' is prepared to give real power to the neighbourhoods, in other words to democratise the process in a way which will provide a really radical new approach to service delivery. All the doubts still exist about whether the people of the borough really want power, or are equipped to use it, about whether the interests of the minorities can be safeguarded and about whether departures from centrally-determined service standards can be accommodated. There are doubts too about the ability of staff at neighbourhood level to take up the challenge. When things start to go wrong in local government, the instinct of leading politicians and chief officers is still to impose discipline from the centre, to retreat to the barricades of powerful committees and rigid departmental hierarchies. If service delivery is to be democratised in local authorities, as well as relocated in neighbourhood offices, then the centre has to be prepared to give up power in the interests of real reform from the bottom up. As one of Islington's neighbourhood officers said recently, 'The test is whether individual local officers have room to make their own mistakes'.

Conclusion

We are convinced in Islington that our services have improved, qualitatively as well as quantitatively, since they were decentralised [1]. There have been short-term improvements particularly in repairs, estate management and tackling poverty. There is evidence too of our consumers identifying with their neighbourhood and their office in a way which was unthinkable under the old system. But satisfied ratepayers do not generally make news and we need to follow up the anecdotal evidence with some consumer research. The debate is continuing on how best to democratise the process and share power with the community and it is in this area that decentralisation poses its most severe challenge for the next five years.

Reference

[1] London Borough of Islington, *Going Local. Decentralisation in Practice*, London, Islington Council Press, 1986.

4 THE DELIVERY OF SOCIAL SERVICES

Peter Arnold

In his paper in this collection Robin Hambleton refers to two different approaches to decentralisation — to regard it as 'an interesting but passing fad' or recognise that 'there are deep seated reasons why decentralisation is here to stay'. Whichever position is taken it should be clear from the outset that there are substantial problems of definition, terminology and interpretation which make it hard to identify with precision what decentralisation is for or how it might best be evaluated. In this short paper I review what I regard as fundamental weaknesses in the analysis of decentralisation which has been confined to a few authorities, and address some of the problems which arise in evaluating its impact on the social services.

In the first stages of any account of decentralisation readers are confronted with three impeccable assertations. These are, first, that decentralisation can mean 'all things to all men', second, that it has its precursors, for example, the area management initiatives of the 1970s, and third, that it represents a break with the older traditions of local government and a move towards a more modern system characterised by new political and managerial styles. Other equally impressive assertions follow. Decentralisation should be understood in relation to wider international changes in government and business, and as mirroring a changing power relationship between the central and local state, the bureaucrat or administrator and the client.

At the risk of being accused of excessive iconoclasm I must express a certain disquiet with the first two of these claims. The first — that decentralisation 'means all things to all men' — is all too easily made and, in my view, reveals a weakness of system and classification in analysis. The second — that the managerialist orientation of the 1970s is directly connected to the initiatives of the 1980s — stretches continuity and, maybe, memory in local government too far. The third claim — that old style government is on the way out and a new mode entering — though more tenable, is premature and reflects as much wishful thinking as hard evidence. Despite this scepticism, I would agree that decentralisation represents an important shift in local authority policies and practices, though I would shy from describing it either as a managerial revolution or political panacea. What I am convinced of is that analysis of decentralisation needs to be more sharply focussed and critical. My colleague

Ian Cole and I have written elsewhere [1] that research into decentralisation is unrefined both in its methodology and content, particularly when compared to the more critical assessment of the reorganisation of British local government in the 1970s [2]. This deficiency certainly needs to be corrected.

Problems of research
Before I begin to examine the decentralisation of social services, I think it worthwhile to review some of the weaknesses of contemporary inquiry into the subject. Four points need to be made. First, as a subject for research decentralisation has been analysed for the most part descriptively and from a base of information derived mainly from the London boroughs and large metropolitan authorities. The evidence has invariably pointed to the positive potential of decentralisation and has left to one side inconvenient examples of failure to implement or only partially implement individual schemes. This seems to me a woeful oversight. The political cultures of authorities outside London provide fertile ground for research, even if the styles of decentralisation adopted are more pragmatic and less ideological. Authorities which have failed or have had limited success in their ambition to decentralise need to be considered, as do those which may now be in the process of re-centralising some aspects of service. Second, research has tended to gloss over the conflicts of political, professional and managerial interest which have arisen. Third, there has been little or no attempt at eliciting comprehensive information on the variety of impacts which decentralisation has produced, both in terms of different services — housing, social services, etc. — and the different actors involved — elected members, officers, professionals and clients. Fourth, there has been no real direction of effort towards standardising information and terminology, and in consequence, terms such as 'going local', 'creating patch', 'decentralising' and 'restructuring' are used interchangeably and ambiguously.

Quite recently Ian Cole and I specified three themes for research into decentralisation — internal resistance, management control and monitoring — which we suggest need to be opened up. We also outlined five assumptions inherent in decentralisation which need to be questioned. These are that it:
    breaks bureaucratic power;
    changes officer values;
    increases job satisfaction;
    redistributes resources;
    politically regenerates [3].

At the present stage of analysis it is appropriate to add three further observations. First, analysis of social services and housing has generated uneven hard evidence regarding the impact of decentralisation on the client or consumer, particularly in respect of client perceptions of quality of service and relationships with professionals. Peter Beresford and Suzy Croft's investigation into the community response to patch based services marks an improvement on the generally uncritical ethnographic or case study account which, while worthwhile as a reference point, has contributed little that is generalisable [4].

Second, the important question of the effect which decentralisation has had on professional power, most notably in the social services, and the extent to which it represents an attempt at constraining, even deprofessionalising, the professional merits systematic attention. The different stages of professional development and variation in professional style and outlook between social services and housing makes this a difficult and sensitive area for research, but one which should be opened up further in any overall evaluation. Finally, and this point is made with particular reference to the social services — though one might consider wider issues such as privatisation of housing in these terms — there has been limited evaluation of the importance of decentralisation in relation to other policies and non-local government services.

In respect of the social services decentralisation should be examined in the context of the response to community care policies — an issue referred to by Howard Glennerster two years ago in another Policy Studies Institute publication *Decentralisation and Care in the Community* [5]. The chilling experiences of social services departments in their reaction to care in the community, which have been noted by the Audit Commission, sustains Glennerster's view that there is more to think about than decentralisation [6]. Indeed, one might ask of social services departments whether their primary concern is to survive the transition into community care, secure deals with the health service, and maintain services under severe resource pressure, or to respond to the challenge of decentralisation. Coincidentally, there is a further irony in the present dialogue between social services and health authorities in which professional workers in the community setting are not senior enough to discuss and negotiate these changes but are the first to feel the impact of changes in service delivery as community care policies unfold. This again seems to be a rich and telling area for research, particularly in the light of the added stimulus to professional work in the community provided by the recent Cumberledge Report on neighbourhood nursing [7].

From what I have said I think it will be clear that I regard research into decentralisation as a tricky activity. The preliminary work which has been carried out into the decentralisation of housing has suggested a mismatch between the rhetoric and the reality, as explained in Ian Cole's paper. My approach to inquiry into the decentralisation of social services is guided by two parallel observations, that the range and variability in the decentralisation of social services is greater than assumed, and that the political, professional, managerial and client-oriented promises of decentralisation are belied by a more complex and contradictory reality. When the number of authorities decentralising social services was small — East Sussex, Humberside, some London boroughs — the problems of research were few. As the range and number of authorities has widened the need to set research into decentralisation into a broader national and comparative framework has become more acute. Present initiatives in authorities as diverse as North Yorkshire, Cambridgeshire, Bradford, Oldham and St. Helens suggest rather different approaches and priorities than those which guided the first phase of decentralisation. In these authorities there is a greater emphasis on the effectiveness of service delivery and less on the ideological or politically regenerative dimensions [8].

While there is still a substantial interest in decentralisation, I have been struck by an unnerving absence of hard information on these experiments. Most research workers studying decentralisation would be capable of a rough estimate of the number of authorities which ostensibly have decentralised — probably in excess of 30 — but as yet there has been no comprehensive empirical review of the subject and the actual extent of the decentralisation of social services in England and Wales remains unknown. The major lines upon which an initial inquiry of this kind could proceed should, in my view, incorporate the specific objective of determining:

the scale and extent of the decentralisation of social services through identifying precisely the number of authorities which have decentralised;

the political and managerial impulses behind individual schemes, including a review of the conflicting objectives which have been generated;

the impact of these schemes on organisational and management structures and the systems introduced to monitor and appraise change;

the effect which decentralisation has had on professional activity, particularly with regard to the supposed shift from functional specialisms to area-based practice;

the impact on service delivery and service effectiveness and the commitment to devolve power and control;

the importance of decentralisation of social services in terms of its capacity to generate response in other services;

the impact of decentralisation on community structures, particularly in the context of care in the community proposals.

This is undoubtedly a heavy agenda for research, but without confronting these fundamental issues we are unlikely to achieve a full understanding of the impact decentralisation has had on the social services.

Preliminary review
As part of a wider programme of research into decentralisation of housing and social services I have, with my colleague Brian Ewart, recently begun a preliminary review of the decentralisation of social services in England and Wales [9]. Two stages in research have been delineated, a broad national review based upon a postal questionnaire and a smaller, more intensive investigation based upon case studies. A first stage questionnaire has been constructed to elicit information on the socio-economic, geographic and political profiles of responding authorities; staff establishments in social services, distinguishing between day care, domiciliary, residential and fieldwork services; organisational outlook and structure identifying specialisms, tiers of

management and boundaries; and finally, detail on proposals for decentralising, seeking information from those authorities which may have deferred or rejected the option as well as those which have decentralised. Though this research is still in its early stages it is worth commenting on some of the difficulties which have already been encountered.

The first observation is that the quality of information on staff establishment varies markedly, and returns from local authorities show that some social services departments are unable to disaggregate information on staffing to enable us to distinguish between ratios of qualified to unqualified staff in different parts of the service. Clearly this data is important if an assessment is to be made of staff changes and staff skills and the interaction between decentralisation and (de)professionalisation. However, among social services departments which have decentralised finer grained data is available and there is evidence that fuller management audit has taken place.

Second, the boundary definitions given to Division, District, Area and Neighbourhood vary from authority to authority, and because of this it is hard to determine the most appropriate scale for the decentralisation of social services. Though adjustments can be made in analysing data and terms there are signs of variation in the perception of these terms by practitioners and managers. For the purposes of research, employment of a common terminology would be useful, but what we may be observing is an ambiguous perpetuation of boundary definitions from older systems and the inadequate working out of new ones. We wait to see whether there has been an application of terms such as patch and neighbourhood to organisational structure without clear changes in operational practice.

The third observation concerns the actual concept of decentralisation and the level at which it has been implemented. Some authorities describe themselves as decentralised when their decentralisation has been partial. One important element to be analysed is the level at which decentralisation has taken place in the structure and how far an integration of separate services or functions has followed. This integration, where it occurs, denotes a degree of decentralisation greater than where decentralisation is more selective. It may be that in some authorities decentralisation has resulted merely in the provision of more service points and little change in professional practice or procedure [10].

Consumer view
In his paper Robin Hambleton refers to the 'consumerist' approach to decentralisation, a theme of undoubted importance. It is generally held that one of the first consequences of decentralisation is an additional demand on services. In the case of the social services a further 'input-output' evaluation and assessment of the way in which workers respond to this new demand is required. While an overall increase in demand might well suggest that members of local communities find it easier to approach the social services, one would wish to insert a qualitative component and identify how social services organisations respond to this demand by additional or modified resource allocation and more efficient working. The mere fact that demand increases is

no guarantee of decentralisation's sucess. Moreover, we should consider that perhaps the consumer response to decentralised service provision is more concerned with quality and effectiveness than control.

It is a reasonable speculation that investigations into the consumer response and quality of service will increase. If claims that decentralisation increases accountability and responsiveness are to mean anything, then the question 'How have services improved?' needs to be answered directly and specifically. An important aspect in this will be evaluation of those improvements internal to the organisation which have occurred. Two central justifications for integration of different activities in the social services under single management structures are the improvements in communication between professionals and the acquisition of broader skills which result. Unfortunately, as in the case of client responses, the key area of professional perceptions and attitudes is under-researched, though it too provides a fertile focus for the study of decentralisation both as process and outcome.

Conclusion

In this short paper I have reviewed a number of issues which have shaped our present understanding of decentralisation and have itemised a number of weaknesses in general accounts of decentralisation and more specific evaluations. At the present stage of development there are unique opportunities for those engaged in social research to influence and improve local services by complementing the ideological commitment and vision of political decentralisation with a full account of the practical difficulties of such change.

References

1   P. Arnold and I. Cole, 'The decentralisation of local services: rhetoric and reality', in P. Hoggett and R. Hambleton (editors), *Decentralisation and Democracy: localising public services*, Occasional Paper 28, School for Advanced urban Studies, University of Bristol, 1987.

2   See for example J. Dearlove, *The Re-Organisation of British Local Government*, Cambridge, Cambridge University Press, 1979.

3   P. Arnold and I. Cole, op.cit., pp.151-2.

4   P. Beresford and S. Croft, *Whose Welfare: private care or public services?*, Brighton, Lewis Cohen Urban Studies Centre, 1986.

5   H. Glennerster in S. Hatch (editor), *Decentralisation and Care in the Community*, London, Policy Studies Institute, 1985.

6   Audit Commission, *Making a Reality of Community Care*, London, HMSO, 1986.

7   Community Nursing Review DHSS, *Neighbourhood Nursing: a focus for care*, London, HMSO, 1986.

8   See for example *Social Services Insight*, 2(4); 2(15).

9   P. Arnold and B. Ewart, *The Decentralisation of Social Services: a national review*, Humberside College of Higher Education, Faculty of Arts Research, 1987.

10   See also P. Hoggett, 'Going beyond "a rearrangement of the deckchairs": some practical hints for councillors and managers' in, P. Hoggett and R. Hambleton, op.cit., p.159.

5 THE DELIVERY OF HOUSING SERVICES

Ian Cole

Most proposals to decentralise local authority housing services over the past few years have incorporated an explicit commitment to make housing management more effective, responsive and efficient. This has often been complemented by other objectives — to extend user control and democratise provision. These dimensions will not be considered in detail here. The main theme of this paper is the success of housing decentralisation programmes in achieving the more effective provision of services, and thereby salvaging an apparently discredited and unpopular local government function from the stream of criticism from tenants, councillors, community activists and, not least, central government over the past few years. I will consider why the objective of better service delivery is so central to the debates around decentralisation, suggest some difficulties in assessing the impact of these schemes and offer supporting evidence from the results of a survey and ongoing information from several local authorities, particularly in the North of England.

It is not too fanciful to claim that decentralisation has come to be seen as a lifeline for a housing service on the verge of terminal decline. Despite the effects of the government's council house sales programme, the drastic cutbacks in capital expenditure, the sharp increase in rents due to withdrawal of subsidy, the growing disrepair of the council housing stock and the virtual cessation of new public sector housebuilding, decentralisation seemed to offer a glimmer of hope for the future — hope that a better service could be provided for tenants and residents. The prospects of achieving a responsive, flexible and accessible local service provided one of the few — possibly the only — positive and dynamic opportunities for public sector housing in a bleak and hostile climate.

In order to appreciate the extent to which the promise of improved service delivery has been integral to decentralisation programmes, it is first essential to recognise the distinctive vulnerability of local authority housing when compared to other established public services such as education or personal social services. The continuation of any major housing function under direct local government control has been placed under increasing threat. These growing challenges to the role of local authorities as providers and managers of rented housing have effectively raised the stakes of the questions surrounding decentralisation. Will it be an effective strategy to regain public confidence, improve service delivery and mobilise greater support for council housing? Or will it eventually be perceived as yet another in a long list of failures, and spell the beginning of the end for local authority housing? One must first outline the increasingly virulent attack on council housing, as a backcloth to understanding how the impact of decentralisation has come to take on such awesome responsibilities.

Council housing in retreat

Local authority housing has always held a rather insecure foothold in the range of social welfare services and has never attained the near-universal coverage of state education or health services. The ideological commitment to private property, the dictates of the market and the subservience of socially informed housing strategies to economic policy have ensured that the claims of collective public housing provision have always been strictly circumscribed [1]. The relentless postwar expansion of owner-occupation, propelled by fiscal advantages and cross-party support, rapidly consigned council housing to a subsidiary role in housing tenure. Furthermore, the low status of housing management, especially when compared to the quicker pace of professionalisation in areas such as social work or planning, fed criticisms about the inefficiency, paternalism and bureaucratic nature of the service well before the election of the first Thatcher government [2].

Despite these shortcomings, public sector housing continued to play a significant role, particularly by international standards. By 1979 almost a third of all households in Britain were housed in the state sector. Since that time, central government's assault on local authority housing has gathered pace. The most visible policy in this programme has, of course, been the sale of council housing under the Right to Buy legislation. The uneven rate of sales across the country means that the eclipse of council housing is already in prospect in more affluent, less urbanised areas in the south east [3], and one million of the six million council dwellings in Britain have now been sold. This strategy has caused the public sector to play an ever more residual role in local housing markets, providing deteriorating accommodation for an increasingly marginalised population dependent on state benefits, concentrated in deprived towns and cities or on stigmatised peripheral estates [4].

It would now seem that this strategy of 'residualisation' in local authority housing is turning into one of outright decimation. The 1986 Housing and Planning Act has eased the way for the disposal of entire estates to other organisations, such as building societies, housing associations or Development Trusts. The recent, carefully leaked statement by John Patten, then Minister for Housing, raised the issue of taking housing out of direct local authority control [5].

Yet if the death knell of council housing has sounded, there are few, it seems, who mourn its passing. The strategy of privatisation has been electorally successful, especially in attracting the votes of the critical group of skilled and semi-skilled manual workers. The extension of home ownership through the

Right to Buy usually takes second place only to the control of inflation in the litany of achievements claimed by the Thatcher government. Nor has the attack on local authority housing been confined to the Right. The Labour Party has shifted its position on the sale of council houses from outright opposition to ambivalent and pragmatic acceptance [6]. Others on the Left have claimed that there is nothing quintessentially socialist about council housing, implying that only home-owning middle class radicals would be romantic enough to defend it [7]. The influential 1986 report by the Audit Commission, which was highly critical of housing standards and housing management, simply added another voice to this chorus of criticism and disillusion [8]. In this climate, it was scarcely surprising that the provisions of the 1986 Housing and Planning Act, which effectively removed security of tenure from five million households in the country, were passed with barely a whimper of complaint.

In short, council housing has become a totem of the failings of centralised and ossified local government provision, replete with misguided investment, unresponsive and inefficient management and remote from the needs and interests of tenants. The cliche of the 'dismal, sprawling, soulless' council estate (the adjectives were changed, even if the sentiment was not) came to act as a motif for all the shortcomings of bureaucratic public services — monotonous, depressing, a monument to local councils' mismanagement and ineffectiveness.

The promise of decentralisation

In the face of this onslaught, it is entirely understandable that decentralisation should become a straw to be clutched by beleaguered local authorities. One of the underlying motives for decentralisation initiatives generally has been to counter dissatisfaction with the prevailing form and content of public sector provision [9]. Decentralisation has therefore been an expression of the reaction against the failures of centralism, rather than a positive alternative strategy forged, as it were, on its own terms. Certainly programmes of neighbourhood-based services often formed part of broader political strategies at local authority level, particularly in councils controlled by the 'new Urban Left' [10]. Yet the focus of decentralisation was still fashioned primarily as a response to pressure and criticism from tenants, councillors, community activists and central government.

The decentralisation of housing services therefore became at once a positive strategy for the future, and an immediate retort to critics. Certainly, the strategy had its limits. Issues such as the design faults of system-built dwellings or the disrepair of interwar housing could obviously not be resolved through decentralisation. The initiatives could, however, address the charges of inefficiency, paternalism or remoteness which had formed the thrust of the attack. It offered a two-pronged strategy — democratising the housing service, while also making it more effective. The fact that decentralisation might comprise conflicting, or even mutually exclusive, objectives was usually overlooked in the enthusiasm to 'do something positive' [11].

This optimistic outlook received further encouragement following one of the most ambitious — and certainly the best documented — programmes of housing decentralisation by Walsall Borough Council in 1981. The Town Hall Housing Department was dismantled and staff and services relocated in a network of 32 neighbourhood offices. The objective of better service delivery was at the heart of the initiative from the outset. It was intended that more ideologically informed aims, such as the commitment to tenant participation and political education, would follow. In the event this strategy was frozen by a change of political control in 1982.

The crucial event in generating wider interest in the Walsall initiative was the public response to threats by the anti-Labour coalition to close neighbourhood offices. David's account shortly afterwards described the reaction as follows:

> ...the coalition is in disarray ... they have been unable to carry out any positive policies of their own and the neighbourhood offices have continued to grow in popularity amongst vital sections of the community. Motions to Council to dismantle several neighbourhood offices have been vigorously opposed by tenants, thereby proving the point that if you provide a service good enough, then people won't give it up easily [12].

The lessons of this response were not lost on the coachloads of councillors and officers turning up to visit Walsall. Here was one local housing service — out of 400 across the country — that tenants actually *defended*! Council housing could be popular. Neighbourhood decentralisation was a way of improving services and gaining community support in the process.

Some of the distinctive ingredients of the Walsall experiment (strong chairman/chief officer commitment, weak trade unions, separate, identifiable communities) were overlooked in the consequent clamour by local authorities with very different characteristics attempting to 'do a Walsall'. Jeremy Seabrook's rather dewy-eyed account of the Walsall experiment provided the icing on the cake [13]. Thanks to decentralisation, it seemed, here was the Walsall working class miraculously reincarnated in its early 1950s version — brimming with self-confidence, solidarity and mutual support, and reinventing close-knit communities.

Improving services
The association between decentralised provision and better service delivery — which had been hoped for, or assumed, earlier — had apparently been confirmed by the Walsall experience. Decentralisation did, after all, offer a chance to rescue local authority housing. The result was a series of programmes undertaken by councils which developed, like Walsall, precise proposals for service reorganisation, but were considerably vaguer on the means of extending community control over services.

This link between decentralisation and better housing service delivery was also essential at a local level in gaining wider support for initiatives beyond a small coterie of committed councillors, officers and party activists. If the 'jam tomorrow' of democratisation remained the ultimate stated objective of going local, it was 'bread today' of quicker repairs and more effective management which would win a readier public response.

The proseletyzing efforts of those involved in decentralisation programmes were, therefore, founded on the promise of better service delivery. The former leader of Hackney Borough Council, Anthony Kendall, probably echoed the experience of many in his account of public meetings held in the borough in 1983 to discuss decentralisation proposals:

> ... the public came in large numbers. Although they were genuinely interested in the idea of decentralisation, underneath I think they were attracted to it by the feeling that services could certainly get no worse and might improve. That at base was what united everybody in favour of decentralisation: a feeling that there must be a better way of delivering our services [14].

The emphasis on service reorganisation first and foremost in decentralisation initiatives — as a basically managerial strategy (whether initiated by councillors or officers) — was borne out by a national sample survey of housing decentralisation undertaken by a project group at Sheffield City Polytechnic [15]. Of the 54 local authorities responding to the survey, 21 were already operating some kind of decentralised service and a further eight were in the process of introducing plans for decentralisation.

When asked to specify the principal objectives behind decentralisation proposals, aspects concerning service delivery predominated over more ideological aims. For example, the three objectives most often mentioned referred to improved service effectiveness, greater accessibility and the need to project a better public relations image for the service. Only eight of the respondents referred to the broader democratisation of the service and, tellingly, only two mentioned the influence of tenant demands as a factor [16]. These survey results should be treated with caution — the respondents were, for example, usually senior officers who might be expected to give managerially-oriented replies. Nevertheless, I suspect that the political promise of decentralisation has in many cases become incorporated into the more familiar language of managerial reorganisation in the name of effective service delivery.

Now, six years on from the Walsall experiment, a more chastened view is emerging about the potential of decentralisation strategies to regenerate local authority housing services. Progress has undoubtedly been made in many areas. The network of 24 neighbourhood offices in Islington, for example, stands as a genuine achievement based on elected member and officer commitment and tenant support. Other, less publicised initiatives, such as Bradford's, also deserve mention. Elsewhere, from Sheffield to Southampton and from Edinburgh to Tower Hamlets, councils are in the process of implementing neighbourhood-based programmes of varying scale and ambition. Nevertheless, housing decentralisation has not been good news all the way. London boroughs such as Hackney, which formulated politically adventurous plans, have run into difficulties due to a variety of internal and external pressures. Seven years of struggle with declining resources, central government controls, ratecapping, deteriorating stock, increasing homelessness and intensifying social problems have taken their toll in many areas. Councillors and officers are not asking 'how will decentralisation improve the housing service?' any more; they are asking 'how much will it cost to improve the service?' and 'how can we tell if the service has improved?' The answers to both these questions are proving difficult to come by.

Monitoring the impact of decentralisation

The national sample survey asked local authorities the extent to which the objectives of decentralisation had been achieved. The results suggested an encouraging picture — a third of respondents said the objectives had been 'very well' achieved, a third said 'quite well' and the remaining third felt it was too early to say or did not reply. Nowhere had decentralisation been perceived as a failure.

These survey responses in fact prompted further questions — on what grounds were these judgements being made? How could 'success' or 'failure' be measured? What criteria were being used? These questions are especially important in view of the wider interest in the experience of those local authorities which have embarked on decentralisation programmes. In fact, only a minority of the local authorities were specifically monitoring the impact of decentralisation, and even then in a fairly rudimentary way, usually through analysing voids and arrears statistics.

One should not be too surprised at these figures — the information base in many housing departments is extremely weak and, in the face of cutbacks in resources, it is entirely understandable if councils concentrate their attention of improving front-line services at the neighbourhood level rather than developing more sophisticated and analytical research and monitoring techniques. Yet it is still disappointing that the effects of such major programmes of service reorganisation are being assessed only on the basis of entirely intuitive and subjective perceptions.

This, of course, begs the question of what a more comprehensive evaluation of the impact of decentralisation would entail. There has been a flurry of interest recently in the development of statistical indicators to monitor performance in housing departments, stimulated by the publication of the Audit Commission's report *Managing the Crisis in Council Housing* [17]. On the basis of a detailed, comprehensive survey of local housing authorities in England and Wales, the Commission devised a range of indicators to reflect the three objectives of service provision — economy, effectiveness and efficiency. The 'economy' measure assessed different staffing levels devoted to housing functions, 'effectiveness' included information on lettings intervals, homelessness, design features and heating costs, and the 'efficiency' measure comprised arrears figures, rent levels, housing benefits and computerised information. In setting a 'benchmark' and a 'cause for concern' for each of these measures, the report produced a composite league table of management performance in local authorities.

The Commission's report has been criticised, with some justice, for its arbitrary selection of indicators, inconsistency and the implicit equation between 'efficiency' and 'low cost' [18]. Nevertheless the Commission's main conclusions — about the poor quality of management information, the lack of direction in organisations and the negligible amount of evaluation into service provision — must have struck a chord in many local authorities.

Strangely, in a report filled with emphatic criticisms and crisp judgements, the Audit Commission is rather coy about the impact of decentralisation on service delivery. The assessment of neighbourhood-based management is somewhat enigmatic:

> In principle, the Commission favours maximum delegation of authority and responsibility as far down the line as possible. Delegation to the estate level can involve an increase in staff numbers, as small- scale advantages are foregone, but it could also lead to a higher level of service and greater tenant involvement and satisfaction, and in many cases the authorities which most need estate-level management are already overstaffed at the centre and could therefore afford to redeploy some of their existing staff resources [19].

One study which has explored the provision of management information to assess the effects of decentralisation is the study of Coventry by Building Use Studies Ltd., as part of a broader evaluation of costs in housing management and accounting procedures used to monitor housing services [20]. The report puts forward the following key performance indicators:

Repairs
: Number of jobs outstanding classified by priority, status, type and neighbourhood.

Rent arrears
: Current list of tenants in rent arrears, with amount of individual arrears and number of weeks in arrears, classified by neighbourhood and smaller property unit (e.g. estate).

Rent arrears totals classified by neighbourhood, smaller property unit (e.g. estate), property type (e.g. semi-detached), family type, and time period (week, month).

Arrears data set alongside housing benefits data for individual cases is also considered important.

Allocations
: Numbers of applications for housing on particular areas, neighbourhoods and estates, per time period.

Numbers of offers made, accepted or refused per neighbourhood, estate or other property unit, per time period.

Voids
: Numbers of void properties and duration of voids per neighbourhood, estate or other property unit.

Analysis of void costs in terms of lost rent and damage to property.

This list certainly provides a much more comprehensive set of indicators than that used by most local authorities in the process of decentralising, and suggests ways in which impact can be precisely measured. What it does not overcome, however, are some of the underlying weaknesses in depending on statistical indicators of this kind in providing any basis for assessing changes in the quality of the service to tenants — which is, after all, what decentralisation is all about.

One of the most apparent shortcomings of performance indicators is that they accentuate the quantifiable aspects of service provision at the expense of less tangible, but equally important goals. As a National Consumer Council report in 1983 put it:

> Some aspects of service delivery are not readily reduced to numbers, or at least to indicators that can be used to compare performance between authorities. This is especially true with service quality and satisfaction ... It would be unfortunate if local authorities devoted all their efforts to improving performance that can be quantified, and ignored other aspects which may be just as crucial. In this case, the process of measurement would start to dictate policy [21].

The dangers of assessing impact on the basis of narrowly conceived, management-determined measures are compounded by other difficulties. How can potentially competing priorities be reconciled? One way of reducing the number of empty dwellings in an unpopular neighbourhood, for example, might be to relax the rules covering allocations to those in rent arrears, thereby increasing the arrears ratio. How is the different weighting of each performance indicator to be determined? Furthermore, how are trends in performance to be interpreted?. A reduction in void properties may simply reflect increased pressure on the housing waiting list, for exaple, rather than improved management effectiveness. In a decentralised service, slavish adherence to key performance measures may also produce unhealthy competition between neighbourhoods, with each local manager striving to improve his or her 'score' at the expense of providing a service to tenants. Elsewhere, Peter Arnold and I have suggested that decentralisation may paradoxically increase the power of the centre, operating on a 'divide and rule' basis between different neighbourhoods [22].

Any monitoring has to be clearly framed within an appraisal of differential costs to the organisations. A drive to reduce the level of rent arrears, for example, may start to become counter-productive, if the increased marginal costs of more intensive collection procedures outweigh any gains in increased rent revenue [23]. The additional costs of decentralisation have generally received little detailed analysis by local authorities. Some councils have made calculations of the direct costs caused by building new offices and appointing extra staff. (Islington's 24 neighbourhood offices, for example, cost around £9.8 million.) Far more difficult to calculate are the indirect costs of decentralisation, particularly due to the increased demands for more accessible services. It has not been possible for local authorities to formulate precisely how much extra rent a week would be required from tenants to pay for a programme of neighbourhood-based provision.

Finally, it is essential that the purposes of performance measurement to monitor decentralisation are not wrenched out of their political context, so that priorities become lost or misplaced. As Flynn has pointed out:

> Unless performance measures are integrated with management processes and culture of an organisation, they will become no more than a mildly irritating exercise in the collection of statistics [24].

The use of performance indicators to assess the impact of decentralisation on service delivery can prompt local authorities to ask themselves questions about the overall purpose of the policy — to provide a better service for tenants and residents, rather than become focussed on internal organisational objectives. This may be a healthy reminder about the value of the 'public service orientation' of local government recently highlighted by Michael Clarke and John Stewart [25]. Yet very few councils undertake systematic appraisals on this basis and even then performance measures only offer partial insight into the impact on service delivery, requiring very careful interpretation. These techniques must be supplemented by methods which can explore the qualitative aspects of change in service delivery.

The simplest way to assess impact is perhaps just to ask front-line housing workers and tenants whether the housing service has improved under decentralisation. Obviously, this begs further questions, about extraneous influences on the service — especially resources — which may colour the responses. Yet it is extraordinary how few local authorities have even made tentative steps in developing this kind of dialogue. Some local authorities, such as Manchester, Newham and Islington, have undertaken large-scale consumer opinion surveys concerning attitudes towards decentralisation, and have followed these up with more detailed surveys as part of consultation programmes. Yet overall it is depressing to note how little has been done on a regular monitoring basis. A comprehensive approach would entail periodic neighbourhood surveys, structured and unstructured group discussions with workers at all levels and service users, public meetings, seminars, analysis of complaints data and individual diaries or biographies. This kind of information could begin to chart subjective perceptions of the housing service, map changing expectations and priorities and penetrate the lopsided picture of change produced by statistical indicators for senior management.

The recent National Consumer Council report *Measuring Up* provides a good start in combining quantitative and qualitative approaches to assess the provision of selected services in Cambridge and Newcastle [26]. In housing, this includes the useful checklist devised by Newcastle Tenants' Federation to evaluate the repairs service. Elsewhere, the study by Beresford and Croft of the 'patch' social work initiative in East Sussex stands as a testament to the potential for providing a sensitive, detailed and multi-layered analysis which engages with service users about the kind of public services they want [27]. There is, as yet, no parallel study of tenant responses to decentralised housing services. All this work is very much at an embryonic stage, in urgent need of further development.

Conclusion

One is, then, left with the irony that, for a strategy hinged on responsiveness and accessibility as cardinal features, very little attention has been given to the attitudes and perceptions of tenants towards the impact of decentralisation. Decentralisation is a major departure for any local authority. It is often an expensive initiative, requiring major managerial reorganisation, reshaping every aspect of service delivery, bringing forth new attitudes and ways of working, establishing new priorities and involving service users in a totally different way. Yet it remains quite difficult to say what benefits have been achieved through all this energy, experimentation and expense.

I do not wish to sound unduly pessimistic about the consequences of decentralisation. Indeed, I sense that the misplaced and fashionable euphoria of a few years ago is in danger of being eclipsed by an equally misplaced and fashionable despondency now. The available evidence does suggest that decentralisation has brought about positive achievements. In many areas, the service has been made more accessible, attitudes have changed, better communication has resulted between front-line staff and tenants. However, we need to know much more about how these features are counteracted by items on the other side of the balance sheet — vulnerable and demoralised staff, overstretched services unable to cope with rising demand, spiralling costs, poor communication between neighbourhoods, lack of genuine tenant participation. Yet it is precisely these kinds of evaluations which are required if more local authorities are to be encouraged to follow in the footsteps of the pioneers of decentralisation, through the treacherous terrain of local government in the late 1980s.

It is necessary for local authorities to make significant improvements in their base of information about housing management and to develop more sophisticated monitoring procedures, in order that the impact of decentralisation can be assessed. However, these kinds of official evaluations must be incorporated into much broader accounts, which give priority to the views, experiences and attitudes of front-line workers and especially those local tenants and residents on whose behalf decentralisation was devised in the first place. This is not just a case of reproducing a standard questionnaire in which members of local communities are represented only as isolated and passive 'respondents' to preordained questions, emerging only in aggregated totals in tables of survey results. Fuller, more sensitive and continuous methods of appraisal are needed to achieve effective communication and, as we have seen, few local authorities have really taken these challenges on board.

It remains to be seen to what extent decentralisation can help to restore public faith in local authority housing. If any progress is to be made, it will not however be through bold but vague pronouncements of intent, but through clear-headed and detailed evaluations of community response. In this sense, the need to secure a genuine, ongoing dialogue with tenants and residents is not an optional extra for hard-pressed local authorities. It is essential.

References

[1] See, for example, P. Malpass and A. Murie, *Housing Policy and Practice*, London, Macmillan, 1982; S. Merrett, *State Housing in Britain*, London Routledge and Kegan Paul, 1979.

[2] V. Karn, 'Housing: the newest profession', *Roof*, 1977; M. Laffin, *Professionalism and Policy: the role of the professions in the central-local government relationship*, London, Gower, 1986.

[3] R. Forrest and A. Murie, 'Marginalisation and subsidised individualism: the sale of council houses in the restructuring of the British welfare state', *International Journal of Urban and Regional Research*, 10(1).

[4] C. Hamnett, 'Housing the two nations: socio-tenurial polarisation in England and Wales' *Urban Studies*, 21(4); R. Dunn, R. Forrest and A. Murie, 'The geography of council house sales in England 1979-85', *Urban Studies*, 24(1).

[5] *The Times*, 5 February 1987.

[6] Labour Party, *Homes for the Future*, London, Labour Party, 1985.

[7] S. Jacobs, 'The sale of council houses: does it matter?', *Critical Social Policy*, 1(2); see also M. Cowling and S. Smith, 'Home ownership, socialism and realistic social policy', *Critical Social Policy*, 9.

[8] Audit Commission, *Managing the Crisis in Council Housing*, London, HMSO, 1986.

[9] R. Hambleton and P. Hoggett (editors), *The Politics of Decentralisation: theory and practice of a radical local government initiative*, Working Paper 46, School of Advanced Urban Studies, University of Bristol, 1984.

[10] J. Gyford, *The Politics of Local Socialism*, London, Allen and Unwin, 1985.

[11] P. Arnold and I. Cole, 'The decentralisation of local services: rhetoric and reality' in P. Hoggett and R. Hambleton (editors), *Decentralisation and Democracy: localising public services,* Occasional Paper 28, School of Advanced Urban Studies, University of Bristol, 1987.

[12] J. David, 'Walsall and decentralisation', *Critical Social Policy*, 7, p.75.

[13] J. Seabrook, *The Idea of Neighbourhood*, London, Pluto Press, 1984.

[14] A. Kendall, 'Decentralisation: promise or delusion?', *Going Local?*, No.1, London, Polytechnic of Central London, 1984.

[15] H. Bentley, C. Button, T. Elliott, G. Hortop, A. Morris, G. Reynolds and K. Wormald, *Decentralisation of Housing Services: a national survey*, Internal paper, Sheffield City Polytechnic, 1985.

[16] P. Arnold and I. Cole, op.cit.

[17] Audit Commission, op.cit.

[18] P. Somerville, 'Nero fiddles, while Rome burns', *Housing*, 2(5).

[19] Audit Commission, op.cit.

[20] Building Use Studies Ltd, *Improving Information Systems for Decentralised Housing Management by Coventry City Council*, London, Building Use Studies Limited, 1986.

[21] National Consumer Council, *Measuring the Performance of Local Authorities in England and Wales — Some Consumer Principles*, London, National Consumer Council, 1983.

[22] P. Arnold and I. Cole, op.cit.

[23] N. Flynn, 'Performance measures in public sector services', *Policy and Politics*, 14(3).

[24] Ibid., p.403.

[25] M. Clarke and J. Stewart, *Local Government and the Public Service Orientation: or Does a Public Service Provide for the Public?*, Local Government Training Board, 1985.

[26] National Consumer Council, *Measuring Up. Consumer assessment of local authority services: a guideline study*, London, National Consumer Council, 1986.

[27] P. Beresford and S. Croft, *Whose Welfare? Private care or public services*, Brighton, Lewis Cohen Urban Studies Centre, 1986.

6 THE ROLE OF VOLUNTARY AND COMMUNITY GROUPS

Bob Davies

'Decentralisation' in Birmingham has taken place in the context of a city of approximately one million people; covering 64,822 acres; 14 miles from its northern boundaries to its southern edges; comprising townships that were administratively separate within living memory; and which, having been the hub of a prosperous region built on heavy industry and the motor industry, is now in serious recession.

It is a city that has a well established and dominant bureaucracy built on Joseph Chamberlain's concept of the City Corporation, the political rule of which has oscillated from right-wing Labour to traditional Conservative over the postwar years. It is a city that has little history of community action or radical politics, and the political polarisation found elsewhere does not exist to any great degree.

A brief history

The Birmingham Labour Party fought and won the May 1984 municipal elections on a manifesto that gave a commitment to seeking:

> ... a partnership with residents of Birmingham by providing greater accessibility to the services of the City Council and by giving residents a greater say in the planning and management of these services. [1]

To achieve this the party introduced three main policy initiatives, Area sub-Committees, neighbourhood offices, and the reorganisation of the City's Youth and Community Service.

Area sub-Committees (AsCs) were established across the city, with one in each of the 12 parliamentary constituencies. It was through these that City powers were to be devolved:

> The Council needs to respond to the criticism that it is too remote and insufficiently accountable for its actions. Labour's objective is to involve local communities on a permanent basis in the decisions that affect their lives. Upon taking control, we will move immediately to devolve decision-making functions to Area (sub) Committees.

The core membership of each AsC was to be the elected ward members from the three or four wards in each constituency. In addition, the then County Councillors and the Member of Parliament for each constituency were coopted with full voting rights.

The 1984 manifesto had indicated that:

> ... as an interim measure, residents will be elected to the Area (sub) Committees through an election process involving City Council recognised residents', tenants' and community groups.

However the City Solicitor advised that this was not legally possible and although this advice is apparently incorrect, this system of cooption from the community was shelved. The AsCs were delegated to exercise the functions, powers and duties of the great majority of City Council committees, and were empowered to make recommendations to all of these committees.

The AsCs were to be serviced by committee clerks and support staff organised centrally through the Chief Executive's Department, and by locally-based or area-focussed officers of service committees and departments, particularly housing, urban renewal, planning, social services and recreation and community services.

The AsC initiative was paralleled by the development of policies concerned with the localisation of service delivery and the provision of local sources of information, advice, advocacy, and problem-solving services. These functions were to be carried out by a network of neighbourhood offices (three or four per parliamentary constituency area), based in accessible positions, staffed by officers of the main service departments with quick access to all others, centrally organised and serviced by the Chief Executive's Department.

Unlike many other initiatives of this nature across the country, the neighbourhood offices (NOs) were given no specific community development role, and no operational links appear to have been planned or made between NOs and AsCs in the early stages of the policy implementation.

There is a clear community development function in the third element of policy introduced by the Labour Party from May 1984. For many years youth and community work in the city had been the responsibility of the Education Department. Attempts had been regularly made over the years to reorganise the service in order to maximise resources, and to some extent localise the management structure. The 1984 initiatives eventually drew youth and community work into a newly created Recreation and Community Services Department (R&CSD).

R&CSD was decentralised on to constituency boundaries, with the creation of 12 area-based management teams, responsible for all departmental activities and resources in these areas, including 12 Community Development Officers responsible for work with local community groups and voluntary organisations.

These CDOs have become the 'front-line' officers for that department and its committee (Leisure Services) in respect of voluntary action and join other officers from the Social Services and Housing Departments, the Economic

Development Unit of the Development Department, and Urban Renewal Project Teams, responsible in a variety of decentralised, localised or area-focussed formats for liaison with and the funding of the organised voluntary sector.

Decentralisation and voluntary action
The decentralisation movement in Birmingham has considerable implications for voluntary action.

All Birmingham residents are, at some time or another, actual or potential voluntary activists at a number of levels — as volunteers, members of community or interest groups, participants in local activities and consumers with experience and opinions of the services they receive.

The City Council has presented decentralisation, first as 'one-stop shopping' for council services, enabling direct access to information and speedier and more decisive action; and second as a method of devolving power to local communities. In addition the various initiatives have been heralded as leading to a 'new breed' of local authority officer and better representation of neighbourhoods, and as providing easier opportunities for the community to get what they deserve, need, want and have a right to.

All this appears to coincide with most of the intentions of potential voluntary activists who could be seen as wishing to be involved in the following 'resource transactions':

Resource acquisition — adding to a stock of, and/or increasing access to, particular resources.

Resource improvement — improving the quality of existing resources.

Resource rejection — opposition to and rejection of proposed resources.

Resource conservation — retention of existing resources under threat of reduction or removal.

Resource administration — management of local resources owned by others.

Resource provision — providing and managing resources independently. [2]

The initiatives on decentralisation will have to respond to these demands.

Neighbourhood offices and voluntary action
Neighbourhood offices are points at which, it is presumed, information, advice and action can be gained by residents. They differ from previous facilities by providing a local contact point with 'the powers that be', from a wide range of City Council departments. Previous local contact points for Social Services, Urban Renewal and Housing Departments, all of which were also geographically focussed, provided access on a departmental basis only. Any

cross-departmental work was the responsibility of the consumer to organise or at best was organised between professional staff, often at a point of crisis when significant intervention appeared necessary.

Geographical organisation with local access and contact points may have encouraged a more area-based approach but services were organisationally and centrally determined and were not community-based.

Community-based, community-sensitive and inter-departmental services have not prospered in Birmingham's centralised, departmentalised political and bureaucratic structure. To promote community-based work or inter-departmental cooperation, local authority officers have had to work across departments and professional disciplines. Such work has never had high professional or political priority because it detracts attention from the main tasks and its results are difficult to measure by standard departmental criteria.

This has been very clear since 1973 in the work of the Urban Renewal Programme, whose great promise of multi-disciplinary working was never fully realised, and from 1972 in the history of the Social Services Department's Family Advice Centre and Neighbourhood Centre activity. In both these cases professional, bureaucratic and political pressures have prevented the full achievement through new methods of working of innovative aims.

Much voluntary action derives from the lack of integrated services in the City, and the limited interchange of information between the local authority and its citizens. Advice and information projects and certain intermediary bodies have come into existence to fill gaps in services and resources, or to create opportunities for interchange or to carry out the resource transactions mentioned earlier.

It appears that the decentralisation initiatives are intended to inherit some of these tasks. These moves have a number of implications for actual and potential voluntary action bodies. There is, however, little evidence that the position of the voluntary sector was fully considered when the policy initiatives were being developed and implemented.

The policies that generated NOs took little account of the existence of widespread provision of services similar to, and in some cases identical to, those intended for NOs. Also disregarded was the considerable experience within and outside the City Council on issues of local service provision.

Should the use of neighbourhood offices develop as intended, it is unlikely that the extra demand will be met easily. Even in the absence of excessive demand it will be necessary for NOs not only to be aware of local voluntary sector provision, but also to have arrangements for cross-referral and liaison.

A prerequisite of this will no doubt be greater knowledge and recognition of the work of voluntary groups by the service departments delivering services through NOs. This could mean a consolidation and development of relationships that already exist, transferred to the new local context of work, but these will probably need new policies, generated from the political and bureaucratic framework that directs NOs, to create the necessary legitimacy and impetus.

Area sub-Committees and voluntary action

Since their establishment in 1984 the 12 AsCs have carried out their responsibilities in a variety of ways but in respect of their relationship with local voluntary action they appear to have four main tasks:

Informing — making residents aware.

Consulting — giving and receiving feedback.

Supporting — assisting their activities.

Involving — creating working relationships.

The ability of the City Council to carry out these tasks productively is dependent on a large number of factors. The commitment through stated policy appears to be there in the manifesto and in later policy statements. Some of the AsCs seem to be willing to encourage involvement by members of the public attending the meetings, and also to take account of the contributions that are made.

However, two year's experience of AsCs has shown that the prerequisites for productive and effective working relationships are:

the making of significant decisions at a local level;

wholehearted commitment by officers and elected members;

realistic expectations by councillors, officers and elected members;

realistic expectations by councillors, officers and residents;

change in established attitudes and methods;

resources to support involvement, development and action.

At the risk of caricaturing activities in the last two and a half years, it could be said that the majority of decisions made at AsCs have been in areas of delegation from the City Council's service committees that have no significant financial implications for the City. This does not mean of course that the decisions that have been made are not of local importance. Much of the output of AsCs on planning issues is of great import, as are many of the policy issues that some AsCs have discussed, called for reports on and made recommendations about. But AsCs have little power to influence significantly City activity in their areas; this still remains the responsibility of the main service committees and of the central bureaucratic and political structures.

This is clearly manifested in the behaviour and attitudes of the elected members on the AsCs and the officers that report to them. In many ways the meetings of AsCs are no more than a standard council sub-committee held in public. The traditional methods have been transferred to a local — and open — venue. Although this has resulted in these systems of decision-making being exposed to a larger number of people, the role of such 'observers' has been generally passive and has not had a great effect on the process. Some councillors and officers have developed a more explanatory style, addressing their contributions to the meeting as a whole, whilst others have carried on as usual.

This prevents increased involvement by the community in the work of AsCs. The culture has been transferred to a local level, with its attendant attitudes, methods and expectations, and this sets up barriers to those who do not share that culture.

A further set of barriers is set up by the lack of common understanding about the nature of the community that may wish to participate. The public attenders at AsCs to date could be characterised as the curious, the organised, the 'professional' activists and the politically aware, with the last three groups being very much in evidence. Theoretically the whole community may wish to be involved, participate or be consulted via AsCs. What is more likely, however, is that it will be organised groups that will come forward, as they already have to a certain extent.

But of course the organised community or voluntary sector is not homogenous across any one constituency area, let alone the City as a whole. It is possible to identify four types of organised groups which will have an interest they may wish to pursue:

those that seek to represent geographical areas;

those providing services and activities in areas;

those focussing the concerns of communities of interest;

those campaigning on particular policy issues.

Each of these types will have a different relationship with the City Council and hence their AsC. Representative organisations (for example, tenants' associations, residents' associations, local federations of groups and intermediary bodies) could expect to be treated, if not as members of AsCs, perhaps as automatic partners in consultative processes. Service-providing organisations could expect recognition of their role as 'partners' with the City Council in the provision of resources (including grant aid), whilst organisations concentrating on particular groups in the community or issues could at least expect access to AsCs for their position to be heard, negotiated and acted upon.

There is no evidence that these sort of issues have been considered at all. What debate there has been has concentrated on particular organisations who have asked, or been asked, to provide information about themselves, usually following complaints, uncertainties or requests being raised at AsCs. Also each year AsCs have been asked to comment on applications made by voluntary organisations for Urban Programme funds from the Birmingham Inner City

Partnership. Centrally controlled, this process has been geared to eliciting AsC opinions on applications and applicants in constituency areas, to inform the service committees' decision on sponsorship.

AsCs have responded to issues raised by interest and campaigning groups in a variety of ways, varying from detailed discussion at a meeting, public dismissal, and referral to the most appropriate service committee with or without discussion and recommendation.

AsCs appear, generally, to encourage the work and development of community groups and voluntary organisations. They are, however, very variable in their knowledge of and referral of groups to more tangible Community Development resources.

Voluntary action and resources for community development
The third element in the City's decentralisation policies is the reorganisation of the City's Youth and Community Service and the creation of the Recreation and Community Services Department, which included the creation of 12 constituency-based Community Development Officers.

The City already had similar provision of this type in other departments, with various degrees of specialisation and localisation. These officers are responsible for liaison with and monitoring of voluntary and community groups, particularly those in receipt of grant aid. Predictably they are departmentally based and focussed on the departmental task.

All these officers, including CDOs, are concerned with the 'interface' between the voluntary and community sectors and the local authority as demonstrated by the grant aid process. The work of the CDOs, particularly, has brought to light a large number of issues, particularly in relation to the expectations of the City vis-a-vis voluntary group and vice versa. Also of the officers involved the CDOs have had most contact with AsCs, having to report on Inner City Partnership applications.

CDOs have thus begun to assist AsCs in their stated task of encouraging the growth of community groups, but this has been confined to the fairly limited area of grant-aid and these developments have not been placed in any coherent policy context nor guided by local operational considerations.

CDOs, like their colleagues from other departments with community development and voluntary action liaison briefs, are gatekeepers for resources for voluntary and community groups. Their existence has created more local access points for activists and has given considerable impetus centrally for the need for greater clarity in the voluntary/statutory relationship.

The creation of R&CSD and the appointment of CDOs coincided with moves within the Birmingham Inner City Partnership, which had become the premier funder of voluntary bodies, to give more predictability and form to the whole arena of voluntary sector funding and liaison.

These moves led to the involvement of the Chief Executive's Department in a review of voluntary sector support, and this appears to have galvanised the more senior departmental voluntary action liaison officers into a consolidation of the interdepartmental work they had done within the Birmingham Inner City Partnership and its presentation as at least a model and at most a transferable method for future work.

At the same time the Chief Executive's Department is looking into the concept of a 'Community Strategy for Birmingham' which so far, like the investigations into voluntary sector support, is yet to manifest itself on the political agenda. It is revealing to note that neither of these issues were subject to consultation with the voluntary sector, until pressure was applied to officers, when limited external participation was arranged.

It could also be argued that the growing involvement of the Chief Executive's Department, taking on a more interventionist role, has, alongside the growth of the R&CSD and the Development Department (through its work on the Inner City Partnership and urban regeneration issues), has further consolidated the departmental base and centralisation of the City.

Conclusions

Decentralisation, if it does nothing else, should make the whole range of local authority services more accessible. This can alternatively be done through greater localisation of city staff, which is one essence of the Birmingham initiative. To become effective decentralisation, such localisation has to be accompanied by a shift in the decision-making structures to local communities via elected representatives. To make maximum use of the involvement of local organisations, the political system has then to provide a receptive and supportive climate for voluntary and community groups and actively encourage them.

The Birmingham initiatives have all the necessary elements. They are however insufficiently coordinated, and ironically enough are missing the continuing central political driving force that appears to have been present in other cities. The absence of any real consideration of the position of the voluntary sector, organised or otherwise, in manifesto commitments and in implementation reflects the lack of importance or perceived relevance given to service-delivering voluntary action groups by the architects of, and the key actors in, the policies. This is reflected elsewhere in the doctrines of the 'new municipalism'. It denies the potential contribution that can be made by voluntary activists, a contribution derived from their experience of self-generated community projects and their concept of service-delivery in line with perceived or analysed community need.

The establishment of the first NOs demonstrated this set of attitudes clearly. Not only were existing voluntary sector projects ignored in the limited consultation procedures that took place; so too were other City Council officers already liaising with the voluntary sector. In addition, recruitment for all NO posts was confined to existing local authority personnel, with no opportunity for outsiders to apply although they might have had useful community work experience.

At the same time, by reducing the distance people have to travel, by bridging interdepartmental rivalries through the common task of providing more coherent and comprehensive services, and by bringing local authority officers into closer contact with residents, neighbourhood offices should be able to fulfill much of the policy commitment.

Area sub-Committees, by locating some decision-making processes locally, by spreading an awareness of the validity of local opinion, and by involving residents, have potential for setting a new agenda for local affairs. If assisted in this task by the various community development personnel the City employs, drawing upon the ability of certain departments to analyse the demographic, resource allocation and political structures of small areas, they should be able to generate effective working relationships between the statutory and voluntary sectors and the community as a whole.

The three decentralisation initiatives are, however, not linked at a policy level and their interlinking has been left to develop over time through the activities of implementing officers. This is perhaps not surprising given the size of Birmingham, the size of the bureaucracy that has developed to administer it and the speed with which the initiatives were established.

Dividing the City along its political boundaries is a predictable act of an ideologically inspired set of policies. It is also probably the only practical way to proceed. It does, however, ignore the history of Birmingham as a collection of 'townships' with a 'meaning of place' to its residents and their groupings. The real boundaries that need changing are those internal ones that are part of the 'old municipalism', which has created large self-standing service departments and committees providing significant professional and political power bases for councillors and officers.

The voluntary and community sectors have been largely ignored in the development and implementation of decentralisation policies. This is the traditional 'arms-length' approach of the City Council. There is considerable ignorance about the nature of voluntary action within the City, and stereotypes abound. Thus there is no real recognition of the actual and potential place that voluntary and community groups and their participants could have in developing decentralisation and other community-based initiatives. Thus, though the political and professional processes have brought about a considerable, tangible commitment to decentralisation, they have moved so swiftly, departmentally and introspectively as to lose important opportunities.

References

1   Birmingham District Labour Party, *Local Election Manifesto*, 1984.

2   Adapted from D.N. Thomas, *Organising for Social Change*, London, Allen and Unwin, 1976.

7 DECENTRALISATION AND DEMOCRACY

John Gyford

The message from the discussion so far is that there are more questions than answers on the whole range of issues relating to decentralisation. I think this may be particularly true of the relationship between decentralisation and democracy, because in that field above all answers and evidence are hardest to come by. In some ways that might be expected because, even if one could identify for example universally agreed measures of improved service performance in housing repairs after decentralisation, it would be rather optimistic to expect that one could identify universally agreed criteria of good democratic practice after decentralisation. We would probably all have rather more scope for debate about the nature of good democratic practice than about the nature of good housing repairs. So it seems to be in the nature of things that the debate about decentralisation as a route to greater democracy is likely to prove more open to argument and less likely to produce consensus.

That is not all: in practice the available evidence is simply hard to find. The number of authorities that have pursued decentralisation beyond the point of improved service delivery into greater democratisation is fairly limited, at least if one is talking about a form of neighbourhood democracy that parallels multi-service neighbourhood provision. It is not so true if one looks at particular services in particular localities, because there one could probably find rather more examples of what we might describe as 'attempts at user control' — attempts to involve tenants in certain aspects of housing management, to involve parents in the management of day nurseries or to involve users in the management of community centres. There are probably more examples of such small scale citizen involvement than there are of the broader neighbourhood democratic experiments. And that raises the first question that I want to pose, which is: might it be the case that user control of specific facilities and specific services or parts thereof is a more promising avenue for greater democratisation than area-based neighbourhood democracy?

Political problems

The fact that evidence in the field of generalised neighbourhood democracy is hard to come by reflects the political problems of politicians. This takes me on to the question of ambiguity, by which I mean ambiguity in terms of the commitment of politicians to decentralisation. One interesting question is how decentralisation actually found its way into the manifestos and got on to the political agenda in different authorities. My impression is that it got there in a variety of ways in different authorities. In some cases it got there because there was a very clear political commitment to a radical programme of decentralisation. In other cases it got there because it was one of the only things that people could agree on when it came to writing the manifesto. In other cases it got there almost by accident and rather surprised the leadership of the group when they found it was one of the major commitments that they were supposed to be implementing.

So one has to bear in mind that political commitment to decentralisation, in some cases even at the level of service delivery let alone democratisation, varies enormously from one authority to another. That is a major reason why evidence is sparse, because the basic political commitment to translating aspiration into reality has not always been there. Even if it has been, it has often been accompanied by a certain delaying mechanism: one can find a number of instances where leading politicians in some of the London authorities have argued that you have to get service delivery right first before you move on to democratisation [1]. One is actually seen as in some way a precondition of the other: if you do not provide good levels of service delivery, if you do not have an effective neighbourhood level of organisation for your services, then people are somehow not going to want to participate. It will not be worth their while. I am not altogether sure that that is the whole story. One might argue that it is rather like a political version of St Augustine's famous prayer 'Oh Lord let me be chaste but not yet'. I am suggesting that politicians have somehow wanted to put off the evil day and that an emphasis on getting service delivery right first may have been, perhaps only semi-consciously, a useful excuse for doing just that.

In one or two cases politicians have indicated clearly that decentralisation of services is or ought to be the be all and the end all and that decentralisation of power is not what they are in the business of doing. Tower Hamlets provides an interesting example of that at least in terms of the Labour Party. In Tower Hamlets there is a left-wing Labour group confronting a Liberal majority group which is putting into practice what it regards as radical measures of decentralisation. That has led the leader of the Labour group there to say that the sort of decentralisation that Labour wanted was not the decentralisation of power but the localisation of services [2].

The significance of that, it seems to me, is not merely that it raises the question about how much politicians really are committed to democratisation. It also pinpoints the fact that all these initiatives are taking place in a real world of political conflict. Because of this, politicians, in making judgements about the desirability of how far to go in decentralisation, will be doing so not only on the basis of pure principle but also on the basis of political interest, of reacting to the political battle, of trying to take people with them and trying to overcome their opponents. That surely must have an influence on the way politicians look at the desirability or otherwise of decentralisation, particularly at the more difficult aspects of it such as democratisation.

Who would benefit?
The next question is about for whom decentralisation might be beneficial if it were to go on to the stage of greater democratisation. It is never altogether clear who are supposed to be the eventual actors in any more widely democratised neighbourhood institutions. There is talk of the community or the neighbourhood or the residents, but in fact it is not going to be quite as vague as that. There will already be some actors — and Islington is a case in point, where there are tenants' associations who are already actors on the political scene at the local level and who do not want to be elbowed aside by other, newer, actors. There are political parties. What is going to be the role of political parties in neighbourhood level government? Is there an assumption that they will actually practise total abstinence from neighbourhood local politics? It seems most unlikely. The question does arise whether neighbourhood institutions will become colonised by the existing actors — political parties, tenants' associations, and in some fields of activity maybe even the professions themselves. I digress slightly but recent proposals to decentralise educational administration down to the level of individual schools, although they may well be couched in terms of increasing parent power, seem to me to be a classical recipe for professional syndicalism. The people who will actually win will be the teachers, not the parents or the local politicians. One could imagine professionals as well as tenants' groups and political parties being important actors in new forms of neighbourhood politics.

Apart from the question of who the actors might be, there is also a question to be asked as to what exactly is the appetite for democracy which decentralisation may feed? And that raises a further question related to service delivery. If service delivery is good why should people bother to participate in making decisions about it? I know that in terms of civic virtue they ought to and we are all no doubt implicitly in favour of civic virtue, but most of us in fact are not always 100 per cent virtuous, and that seems to be particularly true in terms of civic virtue.

Conversely if services are bad, and that is said to be the creator of an appetite for participation in democracy, that raises the question of why is it that in order to get a good housing repair service people have to give up their Thursday evenings? So whether services are good or bad I am not clear what the relationship is between their goodness and badness on the one hand and the nature of the appetite for a continuing personal commitment by individuals to participate in the democratic process on the other. And I wonder to what extent activists, whether politicians or people in the voluntary sector or radical professionals, are really trying to recreate existing people in their own image as distinct from letting them get on with watching 'East Enders'.

The limits of decentralisation
The issue of how far you can go with decentralisation seems to me particularly crucial. Since at the moment nothing has gone very far, it is not a question which looms large. Everybody is still concerned with how much further there is to go before that becomes a problem, but it seems to me that there are worthwhile questions to ask about how far can you go for a number of reasons. One of them

is the very practical one about the self-interest of those who already have power. I can remember in the very early stages of Islington's decentralisation hearing one of their politicians say 'The big neurosis that grips everyone is fear of losing control'. He did not mean losing control at the next election; he meant having the whole thing run away and dribble out of the hands of the politicians. That, I think, is a real fear which some politicians do have, that the whole thing might be a Pandora's box and that once you actually opened it up you would not know what might happen. There may therefore be a strong desire among some party politicians to limit democratisation and to retain certain powers at the centre.

Over and above that, politicians may also for ideological reasons want to keep certain issues out of bounds at neighbourhood level: the redistributive questions or questions about equal opportunities may very well be marked out of bounds to neighbourhood level decision-making because of the implications they have for broadly redistributive egalitarian strategies, and that clearly means that there will remain a need for power at the centre in order to handle those issues. But there may also be a need for power at the centre simply to deal with the problem of conflicting claims. The work of Michael Lipsky [3] on 'street-level bureaucrats' is relevant, as is a phrase coined by another American, Douglas Yates [4]. Yates was looking at the experience of community control in American cities in the 1960s and 1970s. The phrase he coined was 'street-fighting pluralism' — the war of all against all in the cities — and that it seems to me is a problem which maximum democratisation might have to face. How would you resolve the conflict produced by street-fighting pluralism if at some point somebody somewhere has got to say A gets it and B doesn't? At some level decisions will have to be made and the question of what those decisions were and who would have to make them is a crucial one.

Accountability

That leads on to the matter of tracing accountability. Clearly, the more power that one were to devolve away from the centre down to the neighbourhoods, whilst retaining some level of control at the centre, the more one would begin to be moving towards a two-tier system of decision- making. One would almost be re-inventing a two-tier local government in what, since the abolition of the Metropolitan counties and the GLC, has become almost a one-tier system of local government.

The reason I think that might be a problem is that decentralisation is not happening in a vacuum: other things are happening too. There is the growth of self-help and of the voluntary sector and there are pressures towards greater privatisation. I sometimes wonder whether we might not fall into the trap of beginning to produce a pattern of service provision that became not merely variegated but increasingly complicated. Whereas the problem that has often been posed in the past is the problem of the individual citizen standing outside the monolithic town hall, might we one day find that the individual citizen was now standing in the middle of an impenetrable labyrinth of decentralised organisations and voluntary groups and private contractors and the remains of the town hall and the whole host of activist organisations, to the point where it became as difficult for him or her to find out who did what under this system as it was to gain access to the town hall? That is speculation, but it is something which I think could prove a problem, particularly if it is the case that in many ways society is becoming more diverse, more variegated, more fragmented than it was a generation ago. If one has that sort of vision, and one bears in mind the image of street-fighting pluralism, the problem might loom large of how people would find out who did what, who decided what, who represented whom and who was accountable for what.

Experiments

Clearly whatever mechanisms were being devised for greater democracy under decentralisation this would be an area in which one might expect to find experiments taking place in a rather ad hoc fashion. Since any new institutions are not formally part of the structure of local government, they are not bound by existing statutory requirements relating to the Representation of the People Act, etc. and the composition of councils. And so one would expect to find, and one does find, different experiments in democracy. I suppose one could go back to the neighbourhood council experiments in the 1970s as early forerunners of this, with neighbourhood councils which were in some cases elected, in some cases chosen at public meetings, in some cases composed of people from different groups in the community. That sort of experimental democracy is something which we can begin to see emerging in some contemporary decentralisation schemes.

I want to look at two of them briefly to illustrate a particular point. The two examples are Islington and Tower Hamlets. In many ways, at least on paper, they have devoted more thought to this than perhaps some of the other authorities. In Islington the model for democratic experiment in the new neighbourhood forums has, as one of its components, the notion of ensuring representation for particular groups in the community, particularly those who would otherwise be underrepresented by the traditional process of electoral democracy. There would thus be attempts to ensure that the disabled, blacks, elderly, women and young people were either elected or nominated by groups through some approved mechanism.

If one turns to Tower Hamlets, where they are beginning with the process of setting up neighbourhood residents' forums, what one finds there is a reliance on the traditional mechanisms of electoral representation but with the particular characteristic that, where there were sufficient candidates to warrant it, use would be made of proportional representation. What seems to me interesting about those two different approaches is that they reflect the political stances of the ruling political parties. In Islington a Labour commitment to equal opportunities and a generally redistributive politics leads to a notion of democracy which attempts to redress the representational imbalance arising through conventional electoral politics, by in effect reserving seats for specified disadvantaged groups. In the case of Tower Hamlets a Liberal Party committed to electoral reform identifies a local mode of representation which includes proportional representation. The significance, I think, of those two examples is that democratisation in each case is bound up with the wider political strategies of those two parties. It is not simply or solely to be seen as a response to the particular local circumstances; it is also part of the broader political strategies of the parties.

Conclusion

In one sense decentralisation both at the level of service provision and of greater democratisation is part of a number of changes taking place across society at large. I am intrigued by Paul Hoggett's notion that it may relate to 50-year Kondratiev cycles [5]; I can see that there is evidence for that in some ways. It certainly seems to me to relate to some fundamental changes in society over the last generation or so: a more assertive public, more differentiated interest groups, a much more determined effort by particular sections to stand up for their own interests. Over and above those factors, however, what is happening often also reflects the existence of different political strategies by the political parties and different concepts of democracy in different parts of the political spectrum. That reminds me of an observation made earlier on in the decentralisation debate by Kevin McDonnell when he said that decentralisation is politically neutral and that what is crucial is the political philosophy behind it [6]. The same might be said particularly of decentralisation as a route to democratisation. Part of the explanation for what has happened or not happened in that respect must be sought in the particular political philosophies, political strategies and political struggles that can be found in the localities concerned as well as in more general changes in society at large.

References

1   T. Millwood, quoted in *Going Local*, No.3, 1985.

2   C. Shawcroft, quoted in *Tower Power*, Tower Hamlets NALGO journal, Summer 1986.

3   M. Lipsky, 'Toward a theory of street-level bureaucracy' in W. Hawley and M. Lipsky (editors), *Theoretical Perspectives on Urban Politics*, Englewood Cliffs, New Jersey, Prentice Hall, 1976, pp.196-213.

4   D. Yates, *The Ungovernable City*, Cambridge Massachusetts, MIT Press, 1977.

5   P. Hoggett, 'A long wave to freedom?', *Chartist*, No. 106, 1985.

6   K. McDonnell, 'Decentralisation: progress in London', *Local Socialism*, January/February 1983.

8 CONCLUDING COMMENTS
Nicholas Deakin

I would like to redefine the role that was allocated to me — summing up the discussion and throwing out challenges — and act as a kind of disc jockey. I want to give another spin to one or two of the tunes that we have heard already. They are simply those that I like myself — a personal choice.

The tune I have been most interested by is the blast from the past, the notion that we can replay some of the experience of the sixties and early seventies and learn from it. It raises the question in my mind: why have we not gone back to that rather rich experience before? Perhaps the reason is that some of the lessons that we would learn if we did go back are rather inconvenient. For example, there are lessons about the political stresses involved in the devolution of power, the way in which the people who run decentralised organisations are caught between the pressure from the top and the pressure from the bottom. David Donnison wrote very interestingly about this, and his essay on what were called 'mini town halls' in the early 1970s is well worth resurrecting[1].

Then there are questions about the potential of community development. In the discussion several people have resurrected the concept of community development as a means of getting through to the question of re-empowering the people. In its earlier form, that became a politically very controversial issue; some people may remember that Wandsworth had a community development scheme of precisely that type in the seventies. That, too, raised issues that were inconvenient so they got shelved.

There is also considerable past experience of neighbourhood councils. Again, several local authorities — Lambeth, I remember well — had networks of neighbourhood councils in the seventies, and these raised all the issues about overloaded agendas and the inability to get the public involved in what was going on that we are now discussing. Some of those half-forgotten issues from the past are well worth resurrecting in the present.

Next the question of motivation. Who now wants decentralisation and why? Must it be because what went before was so lousy? I am not very happy with that one. The notion that we can now say to people 'Trust local government, everything has been dreadful before, but now there's a new dawn and we're all born again and things are going to be better than they were' seems rather unconvincing — even dangerous.

Alternatively, we may want it because it provides our social services with a human face. But do people really want a human face on all their local government services? Some of the evidence from the private sector which has been touched on suggests that people might like impersonal services, provided they are efficient. We are rather a shy and diffident nation in many ways. We do not really like the 'You-all have a nice day, do you hear now' kind of approach. There may be a case for impersonality.

Consumer interests
There is certainly and obviously a case for efficiency and better standards in service delivery. That one keeps bobbing up, and it is a tune I particularly like to hear. I gather from Gerry Stoker that I am a consumerist — he has labelled me as such in a recent publication [2]. I am glad to wear that particular label. But there is a question about how efficiently consumerism has delivered the goods in the context of decentralisation. We have heard claims from Liz du Parcq about anecdotal evidence that better standards of delivery have been achieved. We have had Peter Arnold saying this has not been proved. But the fact that it has not yet been proved does not mean that it cannot be achieved. This is an important debate that should be continued and more securely founded on evidence. How does decentralisation in fact improve things for the consumer? One key question here is the one of scale. I am surprised in some ways that this theme has not come up more often during the course of the debate, because some people have argued that breaking up large units of government is a meritorious act in itself. You may remember, this is going back only to the beginning of the 1980s now, Michael Young writing a pamphlet in which he proclaimed in the title that 'bigness is the enemy of humanity' — presumably, to be crushed, as such [3]. I am not sure that I can accept that argument. I think that small, so far from always being beautiful, can sometimes be downright ugly. Small units can be inefficient. They can deprive people of choices and they can be of poor quality. The one thing that you can say about scale is that it may enable you, whoever you may happen to be, to take control more easily. Control, though, to what purpose?

Another tune I am very glad to have heard today is the question of resources and the importance of properly resourcing decentralisation. What does it profit you to achieve socialism in one polling district if the only outcome is competition in misery between the miserable. The preconditions, it seems to me, for success in these experiments — at least in the consumerist definition — are adequate funding (though heaven knows that is crying for the moon at the moment) and also the capacity to manage reources locally. We have not heard a lot about that, not just decentralisation of authority but decentralisation of capacity, of financial management capability (if you like that term) backed by the use of information technology and skills that go along with that.

Consumerism is not enough, Robin Hambleton said at the beginning — a kind of middle of the road number we can all sing the chorus to. Democracy is another story, a musical cacophony really, all those tunes blaring out — the Red Flag and Purcell's Trumpet tune together. Here it seems to me that John Gyford was right in saying that most forms of citizen control decentralisation are pretty clearly driven by different political objectives, and the variety that we see among them goes back to the question of political motivation.

Democracy
We have also talked a good deal about whether politicians can, or indeed should, surrender power — whatever that may happen to be — or control. We were offered some reasons why they might not. Someone said because they were exhausted, others because they never had it in the first place. I am inclined to think that when we talk about empowering we should be talking as much about those who are receiving the power as about those who may or may not be giving it up; both sides of the equation. I do think there is a finite quantity of this substance, whatever it may be, and that it is difficult to see elected members giving up more than a proportion of their power. It reminds me rather of my god-daughter's attempt to train her dog to be a vegetarian. The poor animal knew it ought to eat those awful nut cutlets, but what it really wanted was the red meat. Why should politicians not want the red meat of power? That is what they put in their wet and weary evenings on the doorstep to acquire. It is in their very nature. The politicians like power. I think we have to accept that. But what we do not have to accept is politicians who use the political mandate as a means of rubbishing those to whom they might otherwise surrender some power. I wish I had a few bob for every time when I have been witness to the scene where the politician accuses the community representative of not being elected. 'Who elected you, what is your mandate and where is your accountability?' That is a theme in almost every public consultation meeting I have ever attended.

But if we want a different sort of democracy, a participative democracy, we have to go beyond the purely representative principle. I entirely agree with Bob Davies's line on that. A broader kind of participative democracy is essential if we are talking about power sharing, and we have to talk about power sharing if we take this kind of citizen control model of decentralisation seriously. I very much liked the point made in the discussion about ball games — different ball games going on simultaneously. The participatory democracy ball game is rather like those medieval football matches where whole villages turn out and compete in kicking the ball and each other until the ball lands in the stream. Other kinds of ball games are likely to end up with a variety of different outcomes, as John Gyford pointed out, depending upon the context — whether we are talking about an urban authority or a rural authority, inner city or prosperous suburb

Models of decentralisation
Another question here is about different models of decentralisation and their implications for research. Several people have referred to the way in which models of decentralisation have been bought off the peg, so to speak, and applied regardless of local variations. That may be good for the point of view of research evaluation, but it is not so good for the clients, customers, consumers, citizens, whatever you wish to call them. We need variety in this area because local circumstances will determine local needs, and from the research point of

view I think we need a range of evaluated options which match particular needs.

The 'bottom-up' view is the one which Peter Willmott urged on us at the beginning of this seminar. I suspect that if we were to ask the people about decentralisation we would find that the response might be a bit thin. I think that very often an issue like decentralisation which greatly agitates the chattering classes like ourselves probably begins to seem much less clear-cut when we get down into the localities and to concern ourselves with people's immediate and pressing needs. The test of success that most people will apply to decentralisation policies might not be exactly the same as the ones we here apply. One key test that anyone would be likely to apply is whether the local decentralisation scheme has secured them better service delivery. But I suspect that the question that most people will have to ask is not how the service was delivered or even when it was delivered but whether it was delivered at all. It will be as basic as that, and I am concerned that decentralisation does not have very much to say about some crucial issues, at least in the inner city context, like the race issues that we have barely touched on today, the issue of poverty which Liz du Parcq was the only person who talked about, the question of homelessness which several people have referred to. Decentralisation does not really address those sorts of issues head on. Perhaps it should not do so, perhaps it is not a device which has very much to give in those sorts of directions.

The future
Decentralisation for me remains a focus of interest, even excitement, but something that has not yet realised its full potential. But I would like to think that it could do, and I thought I would end by looking ahead rather speculatively and see if I could identify ways in which decentralisation might develop over the next few years.

We might see a kind of Alliance-tinged welfare pluralist line developing, where local government makes an exit from some forms of service delivery, probably rather an untidy exit in the case of housing, where we might nonetheless get the decentralisation under the user-control banner. So you would have decentralisation not within local government structures but linking residual local government structures to other forms of local service provision, including privatised ones. I can certainly see a managerialist form of decentralisation surviving, and even flourishing, because I agree with those who have said that the bureaucracy has in many places welcomed decentralisation, embraced it even, and used it to enhance professional power. I can see the emergence of a new sub-profession. Is there an Association of Neighbourhood Officers yet? If there is not, there is bound to be one in the near future. I can anticipate discussions on setting up training programmes: we have had them already during the course of the seminar. And I can certainly see very serious discussion of stress and burn-out at the neighbourhood officer level, which seems to me an immediate and important practical problem. But lurking underneath this kind of managerial decentralisation is a covert recentralisation, centred round an enhancement of the role of the chief executive, not concealed by a flimsy top dressing of area sub-committees. I cannot see much more development down the political line, towards citizen control. But I could easily be proved wrong: there is still quite a lot of momentum behind the more explicitly political approach.

Finally, and almost too far over the horizon to see, we might see a populist form of decentralisation — a genuinely bottom-up decentralisation, fragmentary, partial, characterised by immense variety depending on local circumstances, but wanted and valued by people who have fought for it. That is where the community development argument might come into its own: people actually being helped to empower themselves on their own terms and their own definition. That is an implausible scenario, but I would like to include it to cover the range of possibilities. Or else, finally, decentralisation may simply fade off the agenda altogether, and leave behind it, only 'a faint melodious hum', all that is left of the noisy and agonised debates we have had in groups like this.

References

[1]   D.V. Donnison, 'Micro-politics of the inner city', in D.V. Donnison and D.E.C. Eversley (editors), *London: Urban Patterns, Problems and Policies*, London, Heinemann, 1973.

[2]   G. Stoker, 'Breaking the statist mould', *Social Policy and Administration*, forthcoming.

[3]   M. Young, *Bigness is the Enemy of Humanity*, London, Social Democratic Party, 1982.